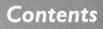

KT-498-397

Contents

The *Revision Guide* series

National Tests Revision Guides are a new series of books that take an exciting visual approach to revision for National Tests. Each topic is summarised in a chart to help you see it as a whole, remember key ideas and understand the links between them. This book is an English revision guide for students in Years 7 to 9 of secondary school who are working through Key Stage 3. It is especially targeted at the tests that all students have to take at the end of Key Stage 3.

Attainment Targets and levels

The content of each subject in the National Curriculum is divided into a series of target areas. These are called Attainment Targets. An example of an Attainment Target in English is Reading.

Each Attainment Target is divided into eight levels and the National Curriculum provides a detailed description of the skills and knowledge which a student should be displaying at each level. So, during the learning process it may be said that some students are working at a particular level and others are working towards a particular level (but have achieved the one below).

On average, students are expected to advance one level for every two years they are at school. By the end of Key Stage 3, when they are 13–14 years old, most students should have reached levels 5 or 6, although some may be working at levels 4, 7, 8 or even 8+. The diagram below shows the range of levels at the ends of Key Stages 1, 2 and 3.

Legend:
- □ Exceptional performance
- ■ Exceeded targets for age group
- ○ Achieved targets for age group (working at)
- ● Working towards targets for age group

	Level 8+	Level 8	Level 7	Level 6	Level 5	Level 4	Level 3	Level 2	Level 1
7 years						□	■	○	●
11 years				□	■	○	●	●	●
14 years	■	□	□	●	●	○	○	○	○

The National Tests

The National Tests (also known as SATs) are intended to let parents, students and teachers know how the student is doing in relation to National Curriculum Attainment Targets. They are designed to find what level of attainment a student has reached in the core subjects of English, Mathematics and Science. The score that a student achieves is converted directly into a level. This is the result that is given to students and parents (or other carers).

About this guide

This guide contains the key points and main ideas of English at Key Stage 3. It revises work you are doing in class and does not attempt to teach new material from scratch.

Each important topic occupies a single page or double-page spread. Some key points are listed at the top of the page. These are then expanded in the chart below, showing how ideas are linked. The margins contain further information, ideas for you to try out, questions and tips to help you improve your English and advice on revision methods. Illustrations also aid visual memory.

It is not intended that you should work through the book from start to finish. Rather, the book is a resource to dip into to find out more about particular topics. Topics you find difficult can be revisited as many times as necessary.

national TESTS
revision guide

English

revision guide

13-14
YEARS

Key Stage 3

First published 2000
exclusively for WHSmith by

Hodder & Stoughton Educational
338 Euston Road
LONDON NW1 3BH

Text and illustrations © Hodder & Stoughton Educational 2000

All rights reserved. No part of this publication may be reproduced or
transmitted in any form or by any means, electronic or mechanical including
photocopying, recording or any information storage and retrieval system,
without permission in writing from the publisher

A CIP record for this book is available from the British Library.

Text: Ron Simpson
Illustrations: Clive Wakfer
Developed by Topics The Creative Partnership Ltd, Exeter

Acknowledgement
The extract from A Walk around the Lakes by Hunter Davies, published in
1979 by Weidenfeld & Nicolson, reprinted in Hamlyn Paperbacks in 1980, is
reproduced with permission.

ISBN 0-340-78992-1

10 9 8 7 6 5 4 3 2 1

Printed and bound in Great Britain for Hodder & Stoughton Educational by
Hobbs the Printers, Totton, Hants.

The chart can be used in a variety of ways, by:
- learning a small section at a time, covering up the section and checking if you know the main words and ideas;
- writing out some of the main ideas as sentences or diagrams;
- checking out any ideas you did not know in your textbook or by asking a teacher;
- following a process in the chart as you practise examples, especially in English or Mathematics.

WHSmith also publishes an extensive range of *National Tests Practice Papers*, which make an excellent companion to this series.

Features of this guide

Why you need to know this.

This section tells you the key ideas you need to know and understand.

The main part of the page builds on the key ideas and shows how they relate to one another.
- It provides examples of how the key ideas work.
- It gives you more explanation of the key ideas.
- It gives you meanings of main words or processes involved.

Story writing

Why does this matter?

When you write a story, you must interest your reader, but you should also try to control his or her reaction.

- Dialogue adds to interest, but it also tells the reader what to think about the characters.

- The diction you use can tell your reader to laugh/cry/concentrate/become anxious etc.

Try this!

Continue **Story B** until Claire goes to bed. Decide why she goes to bed (sent by father, storms out in fury, just tired) and build your dialogue towards that climax.

Writing

✓ A story should hold the interest.
✓ This can be done by your style of writing as well as by your narrative method.
✓ The use of convincing dialogue (conversation) is important.
✓ The diction (choice of words) should be suitable for the type of story.

Dialogue: three versions of the same incident

A
Claire knew she was supposed to be home by half past nine, but she missed her bus and found herself with half an hour before the next. So she went back to Alison's house and waited.

Eventually it was well after ten when she arrived home. Her mother and father were waiting in the dining room and she could tell that her mother was more upset than annoyed. Her father wanted to know where she had been and seemed to think she had spent the evening with Carl, while her mother worried about the sort of people she might have met at that time of night. After about ten minutes Claire got up and went to bed.

clear   easy to follow   accurately written   boring

B
Claire looked at her watch as she opened the front door – twenty past ten! She decided to put on her most innocent smile and hope for the best.

'Is that you, Claire?' Her mother's voice sounded anxious, but relieved.

'Who else do you think it is! Unless she's brought that Carl back with her!'

Claire opened the dining room door and was halfway through greeting her parents when her father interrupted.

'Do you realise it's nearly half past ten? What sort of state do you think your mother's in? She's been going on for the last half hour about the terrible things that might happen to you.'

'Come on, dad, it's fairly safe at Alison's house.'

'Well, why didn't you phone?' and 'Don't tell me what's safe and what isn't!' shouted her mother and father simultaneously.

clear   characters created   longer than A   much more interesting

54

C
Claire opened the door timidly and heard her father shouting.

'Where have you been till this time of night?'

'I've only been at Alison's, but I missed the bus.'

'You could have phoned – didn't you have your mobile?'

'Never mind her mobile – don't the Colemans have a phone?'

'Of course they do, but I just forgot. Anyway I didn't think it mattered. After all, it's only just gone ten and Alison's parents never make her come in this early.'

'That's their problem. So long as you're living in this house, you'll stick to our rules.'

'But what if something had happened to you!'

'I'd have used my mobile.'

'That's typical – you never think about using it when your mother's sick with worry.'

lively   good idea of character   longer than A   not clear

helps to bring out character

needs to be balanced with narration and comment

makes the writing livelier

DIALOGUE

tells us more about character if mixed with comments by the narrator

on its own can be confusing – who is speaking!

Diction: two versions of the same event

Suddenly Gregory realised that their right winger had slipped a tackle and had a clear run on goal. He covered as well as he could, desperately aware that, with only minutes left, his team's chances of winning the cup were in danger. He forced himself to concentrate, stood firm against the attacker, then dived to his right as the shot came in. Too late; the ball was in the net and the school's hopes were over for another year.

Suddenly Gregory came out of his dream of saving a penalty at Wembley to hear the crowd (three Year 7s) shouting at him. He saw the winger charging towards goal and tried to narrow the angle – unfortunately geometry was never his best subject! The winger scuffed his shot, but Gregory dived dramatically in the wrong direction and the ball trickled slowly over the line.

The diction tells the reader:

take this seriously   *treat this as a comic event*

Writing

55

Keep on track

You have probably read or heard far too much about exam stress. This not only makes you miserable, it's actually unhelpful in your work, so get rid of it if at all possible.

Revise hard, but, if you are behind in your revision, just think:

- if you spend your time worrying about what you have to do, you do nothing;

- if you realise you won't complete your revision, get down to work and only do 75 per cent of it: this is better than trying to rush through it all.

Make it clear!

The more dialogue you use, the more important it is to punctuate speech correctly. There is a section on speech punctuation in **Punctuation** (page 47).

Ideas to help you practise or expand your knowledge and skills.

Revision tips and activities.

Tells you the Attainment Target.

Ways to improve your work.

Reading fiction

Why does this matter?

- It is excellent to read purely for pleasure; it is even better to read for pleasure and to understand the qualities that make the book good.

- Your own imaginative writing should give pleasure to yourself, your parents, your teachers and anyone who reads it. So – learn from the writers who impress you!

In the middle

This page deals with novels and short stories. What do we call stories of maybe 70 or 80 pages?

'Long short stories' or 'short novels' would fit many of them, but the usual term is **novella**.

✓ Fiction is the term for imaginative writing which is not factually true – a 'made-up story'.

✓ There are two main types of fiction: the short story and the novel.

✓ A short story may be very short (even just two pages), though it is more likely to be 15–20 pages and may even be 40 or 50 pages.

✓ A novel is much longer: it is often defined as 'an extended work of prose fiction'.

SHORT STORY
- a small number of characters, sometimes only one named character
- a single plot, often a simple story with a twist at the end
- a constant mood: fear, depression, excitement, fun etc.
- a single theme
- single focus
- planned for one single read

NOVEL
- a long list of characters, often including totally unconnected people
- many plots and sub-plots, separating and joining up again
- contrasting moods and settings
- a main theme, possibly, but varied ideas
- variety
- divided up in such a way that it tempts the reader to return to it

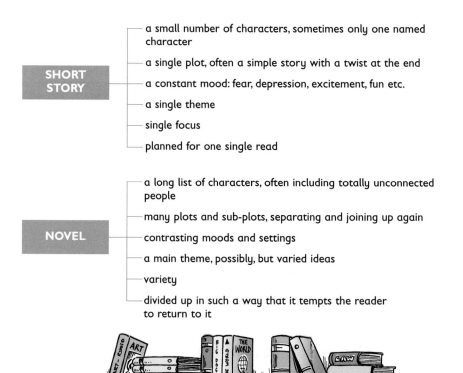

These are not rules on what a novel or a short story has to be like, but what you might expect to find in many novels/stories.

A short story might be praised for:
- keeping the tension throughout

- the way the action is continuous

A novel might be praised for:
- relaxing the tension at times to keep the reader's interest

- its use of 'cliff-hangers' at the end of chapters

Reading

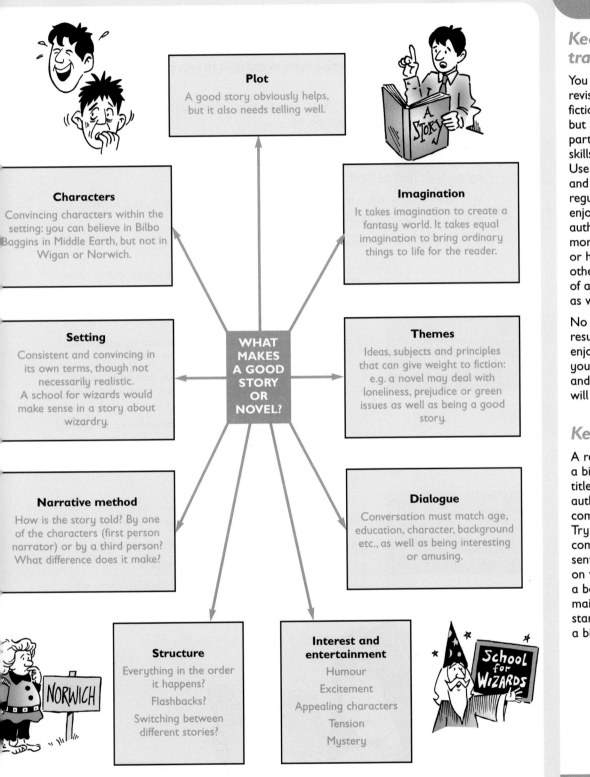

Plot

A good story obviously helps, but it also needs telling well.

Characters

Convincing characters within the setting: you can believe in Bilbo Baggins in Middle Earth, but not in Wigan or Norwich.

Imagination

It takes imagination to create a fantasy world. It takes equal imagination to bring ordinary things to life for the reader.

Setting

Consistent and convincing in its own terms, though not necessarily realistic. A school for wizards would make sense in a story about wizardry.

WHAT MAKES A GOOD STORY OR NOVEL?

Themes

Ideas, subjects and principles that can give weight to fiction: e.g. a novel may deal with loneliness, prejudice or green issues as well as being a good story.

Narrative method

How is the story told? By one of the characters (first person narrator) or by a third person? What difference does it make?

Dialogue

Conversation must match age, education, character, background etc., as well as being interesting or amusing.

Structure

Everything in the order it happens?

Flashbacks?

Switching between different stories?

Interest and entertainment

Humour

Excitement

Appealing characters

Tension

Mystery

NORWICH

School for WIZARDS

Keep on track

You have no need to revise a piece of fiction for your tests, but reading is a key part of building the skills that are tested. Use a library and read fiction regularly. If you enjoy a particular author, look for more books by him or her, but read others (preferably of a different type) as well.

No instant results (except enjoyment), but your understanding and writing skills will slowly improve.

Keep a diary

A reading diary is a big help: note the titles of books read, authors and brief comments on them. Try to make a comment (only a sentence or two) on why you enjoyed a book. 'I like the main character' is a start, but try to go a bit deeper.

Reading

Why does this matter?

Doing well in your SATs
If you know what the writer's intention is (what he or she is aiming at) you have a much better chance of working out what difficult words and phrases mean.

Reading for understanding
Your understanding of everything from newspapers to text books, from advertisements to novels, is helped if you can work out the writer's intention:

• Does he or she want to be taken seriously?

• Is he or she twisting everything to suit his or her opinion?

• Is he or she working on you to buy something you don't want?

✓ The first task in a comprehension exercise is to work out the basic meaning of the passage.

✓ You must be able to find your way through the passage, working out what connects its different parts.

✓ You then need to understand the writer's intention. Does he or she want to describe, tell a story, argue a case or persuade his or her readers to agree with him or her?

✓ You need to consider the 'audience' for the piece: who does the writer expect or want to read it?

HOW TO UNDERSTAND A PASSAGE

Read fairly quickly – identify the subject matter of the whole passage

Pause and think – what does the writer seem to think of his or her subject?

Examine – look at the opening of each paragraph – can you follow the writer's point of view throughout?

Read carefully – identify audience, look for argument, persuasion and the writer's feelings – anger, admiration, humour etc.

Answer – are you ready to answer questions on fact and opinion?

SIX QUESTIONS YOU CAN ASK YOURSELF ABOUT ANY PASSAGE

What is the writer's intention?

What is his or her audience?

Is the writer making a specific point to his or her readers?

Is he or she trying to persuade them of something?

What is his or her opinion of the subject?

What do the opening sentences of the paragraphs tell us about his or her intentions?

Read the following extract from *A Walk around the Lakes* by Hunter Davies, then ask yourself the six questions listed on the facing page.

The variety is extraordinary. In one small plot you have everything of England: lush pastures, twee cottages, stately castles, romantic valleys, lakeside resorts, hidden tarns, smooth hills, wild fells, sudden waterfalls, open heather, rough moorland, frightening crags, dramatic snow-clad mountain tops. It's nature's miniature kingdom. The peaks rarely get above three thousand feet, but, despite their size, enough people fall off them each year, finding them not as cuddly as they may look. Because of the unusual geological and climatic conditions, you can experience almost everything in a very short space and in a very short time, going sometimes from a Mediterranean heat to sub-arctic conditions in just a two-hour climb. Yet the scale is all so manageable. There is no place you can't escape from and be in complete isolation in half an hour, even on the busiest bank holiday.

I have spent the last year wandering round the Lakes. I thought I knew it well, having been brought up in Carlisle, the area's biggest town, but now I know how much I still have to learn. It was a planned wandering. The Lakes are roughly circular so I set myself to wander roughly in a circle, taking in every famous lake, climbing most of the best-known mountains, visiting the best-loved valleys and villages. I wanted to guide those just beginning and yet satisfy those who already know it well.

Now turn to page 10 for answers to the six questions.

Keep on track

English may require less revision of facts than some subjects, but make sure you understand how to do things.

Understanding
Check with your teacher that you know what skills you need.

Making notes
Note points down so that you can remind yourself.

Practice
Practise your reading skills as part of your revision. Can you get hold of an old test paper, perhaps?

Try this!

Why not see if you can write a short piece about an area you know and like? Try to aim at a particular type of reader, like Hunter Davies does.

Reading

Why does this matter?

Evidence is essential:

- **in your own answers**
  The only way you can prove that a writer is giving a convincing account of his or her subject is to find and comment on details. Think of the evidence that proves that Hunter Davies loves the Lake District.

- **in the work of other writers**
  Whether you are reading a newspaper or doing your SATs, you should expect opinions to be supported by evidence. Without it, there is no reason to believe that the Lakes are beautiful or that certain politicians/ bands/footballers/ fashions are best.

Look for yourself

We have said that *A Walk around the Lakes* emphasises contrast. If so, the words 'but', 'yet' and 'however' are likely to be used. Have a look.

What makes a writer successful?

✓ Is his or her style of writing suitable for the intended audience?

✓ Does he or she make his or her point clearly?

✓ Does he or she develop the argument logically?

✓ Is his or her use of evidence convincing?

Intention?

Davies tells us his intention (to 'guide' readers), but often you must work it out from how writers express themselves. You can work out from his style that Davies also wants to share his love of the Lakes: 'nature's miniature kingdom'.

Audience?

Davies makes it easy for you by telling you (last sentence). Again you often have to judge from the style: some writers in persuasive pieces directly address 'you' (the reader).

Specific point?

This might explain the cause of something or why one thing is better than, or different from, another. Davies makes the point that there is so much variety in a small space.

Persuasion?

This asks the reader to accept a certain view, e.g. fox hunting should be banned. Leaflets, newspapers or speeches may call for action. Davies' piece is not persuasive in that sense, though he persuades us of the Lakes' beauty.

Opinion?

Probably the writer will not say, 'I like/don't like this place/person.' You can detect it from the words he/she uses. Look at all the enthusiastic words and phrases in Davies' first paragraph.

Opening sentences?

The first 'topic' sentence of a paragraph will usually tell us what the paragraph is about. So you can work out from this what the writer thinks the next important point is. 'The variety is extraordinary' is a very good example.

The writer's technique

In many ways the most difficult questions are those that begin, 'How does the writer…?' or 'How successful is the writer in…?'. They ask you to examine the technique of a writer.

Evidence

A statement is easy to make: 'The Harry Potter books are fun' or 'It's great to go on holiday in Florida'. But any statement must be backed up by convincing evidence.

The first sentence of *A Walk around the Lakes* is a statement: 'The variety is extraordinary.'

The evidence for that includes:
- romantic valleys/dramatic snow-clad mountain tops
- twee cottages/stately castles
- smooth hills/frightening crags
- Mediterranean heat/sub-arctic conditions.

Well-informed or ignorant?

Old-fashioned or up-to-date?

Studious or looking for entertainment?

Friendly, hostile or neutral?

Audience

What sort of people are going to read the book? What are they like?

Some of Davies' audience are well-informed but some are ignorant about the Lakes. Above all, though, he expects them to be friendly – look at the friendly way he expresses himself: e.g. 'There's no place you can't escape from…'.

Expression

Is the style formal (strictly correct) or informal (casual, even friendly)?

essay on Shakespeare play?

play set in a family?

story about first day at school?

letter to a friend?

WHEN SHOULD WE WRITE FORMALLY?

job application?

write-up on football match?

report to School Governors?

Generally the style of *A Walk around the Lakes* is informal. For example, 'I thought I knew it well', 'not as cuddly as they may look' and 'The Lakes are roughly circular'.

Keep on track

Plan your time
Make a revision schedule. List all the big topics in a subject, then break them down into manageable chunks. Start early enough, so that you finish revising some days before your tests. The night before the test is the wrong time to try to take in new information. It's probably a good idea to spend the last few days checking your understanding of things you have already revised.

Formal or informal?

Many of the examples given are very clear: e.g. formal report to Governors, informal letter to a friend. What about a story about school, though? Probably a mixture of formal and informal. Or a football report? It depends on whom you are writing for.

Reading

Shakespeare

Why does this matter?

Understanding Shakespeare for yourself is very important:

• learning the teacher's notes is not enough in itself

• you need to be able to think for yourself in the tests

• seeing the play in the theatre or on television will help you a lot with understanding it.

Were you right?

Lady Macbeth's lines opposite mean:

• 'You are Thane of Glamis and Cawdor and will become king, but I'm afraid that you are too kind-hearted to kill the present king.'

✓ No matter how difficult the text may seem, remember that Shakespeare was writing to communicate in the theatre: the text has something to say to you.

✓ Be aware of the context, the words and situation surrounding the lines you are studying.

✓ There will be some difficult words and phrases that you can't understand. Either look them up in the notes in your book or simply ask your teacher.

✓ Work out as much as you can for yourself.

Here are some lines from *Macbeth*. Lady Macbeth is speaking just after she has read a letter from Macbeth saying that the Witches called him Thane of Cawdor (he was already Thane of Glamis) and predicted that he would be King of Scotland.

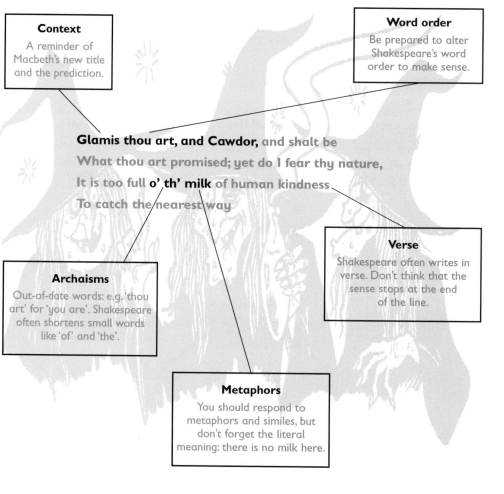

Context
A reminder of Macbeth's new title and the prediction.

Word order
Be prepared to alter Shakespeare's word order to make sense.

Glamis thou art, and Cawdor, and shalt be
What thou art promised; yet do I fear thy nature,
It is too full o' th' milk of human kindness
To catch the nearest way

Verse
Shakespeare often writes in verse. Don't think that the sense stops at the end of the line.

Archaisms
Out-of-date words: e.g. 'thou art' for 'you are'. Shakespeare often shortens small words like 'of' and 'the'.

Metaphors
You should respond to metaphors and similes, but don't forget the literal meaning: there is no milk here.

Reading

• Now see if you can write these four lines in clear, modern English.

12

The following speech is from *Romeo and Juliet*. Romeo has secretly married Juliet despite their families' hatred for each other. He has then killed her cousin Tybalt in a duel and been banished from the city. He is talking to Friar Lawrence who has given him 'good' advice.

The first line is the key to understanding. Remove the archaisms and work out the meaning.

Thou canst not speak of that thou dost not feel.

Wert thou as young as I, Juliet thy love,

An hour but married, Tybalt murdered,

Doting like me, and like me banished,

Then mightst thou speak, then mightst thou tear thy hair,

And fall upon the ground, as I do now,

Taking the measure of an unmade grave.

The deeper meaning of metaphor: this means Romeo is full-length, but it also tells of his morbid despair.

- Now see if you can write these lines in clear, modern English.

What version of line 1 did you come up with?

How about 'You can't talk about what you don't feel'? Very easy, but it's the clue to the whole passage.

Why does Friar Lawrence not share Romeo's feelings?

- Because he is a friar, a holy man, who does not give way to desire.
- Because he didn't get married an hour ago.
- Because he hasn't killed Tybalt.
- Because he hasn't been banished.

That is the **contrast** that the passage is based on: Friar Lawrence calmly giving advice; Romeo tearing his hair and falling to the ground.

Keep on track

Revision is about learning and remembering, but it's also about getting things sorted in your mind. Do you *understand* what you know? Does it all *make sense*? If it doesn't, how are you going to use all those carefully learned facts? Don't be afraid to ask for help if you need it.

Not strictly true

Don't forget that metaphors (not literally true) help with understanding the play: e.g. Romeo's reference to the grave. The Macbeths' guilt and violence are shown in many references to 'blood'.

Reading

Shakespeare: characters

Why does this matter?

Understanding the story of a Shakespeare play is all very well, but you will not be asked to write just about what happens. The other major area you must be able to write on is the characterisation:

- What sort of people has Shakespeare created?

- Do they change during the play?

- How do they react to each other?

- What does Shakespeare want us to think about them?

Romance in Henry V

Comments on Shakespeare's characters refer to the plays *Henry V, Romeo and Juliet, Macbeth* and *Twelfth Night*. You are studying one of these. *Henry V* contains brief scenes of romantic comedy between Henry V and Katharine of France: would their characters fit in with the list of qualities given here?

Reading

✓ Most of Shakespeare's plays have noble, rich or royal people as the main characters.

✓ However, he still creates great variety in characters.

✓ Shakespearean characters may be historically true or invented, tragic or comic, nobles or servants, witty or stupid.

✓ The relationships between them are realistically drawn, even if the situations may seem far-fetched today.

WRITING ABOUT CHARACTERS IN BOOKS AND PLAYS (NOT ONLY SHAKESPEARE)

Age, appearance etc.
This can be useful, but don't overdo it: it is not very helpful just to tell us that Romeo is young, handsome, well-dressed and noble and has a cousin called Benvolio.

Relationships
Behaviour towards others tells us a great deal:
kind/cruel
loyal/unfaithful
rude/well-mannered
snobbish/relaxed

Qualities
The most important section of all. Is the character:
intelligent/stupid?
honest/dishonest?
brave/cowardly?
passionate/cold?
proud/uncertain?

Author's view
Does the author approve of him or her? Are we to take him or her as an example of evil?

Stages in your writing

- Make notes of what you can say about the character.

- Arrange those notes so that you know what comes first.

- When writing about a quality of character, start with a general comment, e.g. 'At the start of the play Macbeth can be seen as a noble warrior' or 'Romeo is unwise because he is too impetuous'.

- Go into details about that and refer to things that happen or are said, e.g. 'He is a trusted general of the King's army' or 'His impatience leads him to buy the poison'.

- Follow it with detail of events or speeches and only then use quotation, e.g. 'Macbeth's status is confirmed by the King honouring him after his defeat of the Norwegian and rebel army:
    And for an earnest of a greater honour
    He bade me, from him, call thee Thane of Cawdor.'

SHAKESPEARE'S ROMANTIC CHARACTERS				
young	devoted	obsessive	witty	poetic
impetuous	clever	loving	idealistic	

Romeo and Juliet

love at first sight

Romeo: love-sick and melancholy for Rosaline

both obsessed with their love for each other

use comic messenger of love (Nurse)

rush into marriage

use musical rhyming verse to express love

can be seen as dramatising themselves and their love

but

genuinely devoted to each other to the death

in the power of others (prince and families)

misunderstandings lead to death

all 'helpers' lead them towards tragedy

Love tragedy

Orsino and Olivia (Twelfth Night)

Olivia's love at first sight for Cesario

Orsino: love-sick and melancholy for Olivia

Orsino obsessed with his love for Olivia; Olivia obsessed with mourning, later with love for Cesario

use comic messengers of love (Cesario and Malvolio)

Olivia rushes into marriage with Cesario/Sebastian

use songs and music to express love

definitely self-dramatising

much talk of death and cutting off from the world, but accept comfortable solution

in positions of power

misunderstandings lead to fights and injuries (of other people) and solutions

Viola and Sebastian arrive and sort out the impossible

Comedy

Keep on track

Learn how the main characters change during the play. You will be studying specific scenes, but the development of characters is something you need to be aware of. If you are writing on Macbeth in Act 1, Scene 7, you must know how different he is from the final defeated tyrant and what signs there already are of later evil.

So revise the play, not just the scene.

Macbeth in love

Macbeth and Lady Macbeth seem very much in love in Act 1 and prepared to do evil to help each other. Love in *Macbeth* is hardly romantic, however. Their unhealthy devotion is part of the process of destroying others and (finally) themselves.

Reading

Shakespeare: characters

Why does this matter?

To understand and enjoy Shakespeare's plays you need to see characters in two different ways:

- in terms of the people and beliefs of Shakespeare's own time
- in terms of their present-day equivalents

You will miss the point if you think that, because of different manners, old-fashioned jokes or supernatural events, they are not 'real' people.

Past and present

You cannot understand Maria, Sir Toby, Sir Andrew, Feste and Malvolio in *Twelfth Night* without knowledge of the role of a jester, types of humour, many obscure references and so on, but the characters themselves are not so very different from those in *Carry On* films. Which part would suit Sid James? Or Kenneth Williams?

Reading

✓ Certain types of character recur in many different Shakespeare plays. It is helpful to examine these types.

✓ This does not mean that Shakespeare just created 'types', not 'individuals'. For example, the unique character of Viola in *Twelfth Night* is a mixture of comic, romantic and heroic.

SHAKESPEARE'S TRAGIC CHARACTERS

Macbeth	Romeo and Juliet
driven by ambition	driven by love
politically powerful	not involved politically
begins in noble valour and cruelty	begin in youthful joy
hangs on desperately to life	sacrifice themselves for love
willing to destroy others	death of Tybalt forced on Romeo
obsessed with himself	obsessed with each other

So no similarity between the characters, but what about their situations?

Macbeth	Romeo and Juliet
at the beginning noble and trusted	at the beginning attractive young members of great families
spurred on by chance meeting (Witches)	spurred on by chance meeting (each other)
frustrated by King's existence	frustrated by family feud
plans and carries out secret murder	plan and carry out secret marriage
behaves in evil and impetuous way afterwards (death of Banquo, Macduff's family)	behave impetuously afterwards: in Romeo's case, kills Tybalt; in Juliet's, risks killing herself
acts on evil advice (Witches)	act on foolish advice (Lawrence)
led into death by misunderstandings (prophecies)	led into death by misunderstandings (Juliet's 'death')
meets tragic death	meet tragic deaths

WITTY

many noble characters (including Romeo and Juliet) show wit in word-play and imagery, notably Mercutio in *Romeo and Juliet* and Viola/Cesario in *Twelfth Night* (scenes with Olivia)

Feste (*Twelfth Night*) is a professional wit, making jokes for a living

Sir Toby (*Twelfth Night*) attempts a coarser wit

CLOWNS

Feste, Peter (*Romeo and Juliet*) and the Porter (*Macbeth*) would all have been played by the clowns in the acting company; so would some of the 'low-lifes' in *Henry V*, probably Bardolph and Pistol

Feste is an elegant, witty clown with many songs; the others are 'clownish' in their stupidity or depravity, though there are still witty comments, and Pistol loves elaborate words

SHAKESPEARE'S COMIC CHARACTERS

VICTIMS

clowns and wits are usually knowingly funny; the victims aren't

Sir Andrew (*Twelfth Night*) is an obvious victim, made fun of for his stupidity and failed wit, beaten up, and robbed by Sir Toby

victims of practical jokes (Fluellen in *Henry V*, Malvolio in *Twelfth Night*) bring it about by their own pomposity

COMIC TYPES

the Nurse (*Romeo and Juliet*) is the 'type' of the gossip: well-intentioned, always talking, not really trustworthy

comic types often work in groups: in *Henry V* there are 'low-life' characters and national stereotypes (English, Irish, Scots, Welsh)

the group at Olivia's house (*Twelfth Night*) combines comic types very successfully: the drunk, the idiot, the comic servant, the witty clown, plus Malvolio as the mocked figure of authority

Keep on track

When picking out quotations for possible use in your tests, choose quotations that serve useful purposes. In the case of a character, try to find a quotation that sums him or her up; in the case of major characters like Macbeth, you need to find quotations that bring out the variety and differences.

Past and present

Romeo and Juliet are probably the best examples of characters we need to see in terms of past and present. All the politics of the city state, the dependence on the Church, duels in the streets etc. are from a different world, but impetuous young lovers separated by families who don't understand are still very much with us.

Henry V: A Heroic Character

Henry V is not a tragic hero and the play is not a tragedy, although his death is mentioned at the end. A tragic hero declines from a position of strength: until his death, Henry V's course is one of triumph.

He is a different sort of hero. Let us call him a national hero. This is a character where we can see what Shakespeare wants us to feel about him. He is an ideal heroic King of England: Queen Elizabeth I, in Shakespeare's eyes, was following the same tradition.

Reading

17

Why does this matter?

You will study at least two Shakespeare plays during Key Stage 3 and Key Stage 4. One of these will probably be a comedy and the other either a tragedy or a history.

See the differences between them:

- a **tragedy** is centred on the downfall of one or two noble characters;

- a **history** gives Shakespeare's version of a period of English history;

- a **comedy** enjoys a complicated and entertaining plot in some warm corner of Europe.

What's in a name?

Tragedies and histories are named after the main characters. Comedies are given titles like *As You Like It*, *Much Ado About Nothing*, and *A Midsummer Night's Dream*. What does this tell us?

✓ William Shakespeare (1564–1616) was the major playwright of the first great age of theatre in England in the reigns of Queen Elizabeth I and King James I.

✓ The plays of Shakespeare (and most of the other writers of the time) are divided into tragedies, comedies and histories.

✓ Well-known comedies by Shakespeare include *A Midsummer Night's Dream*, *The Taming of the Shrew* and *Love's Labour's Lost*.

✓ The comedy you are most likely to study is *Twelfth Night*.

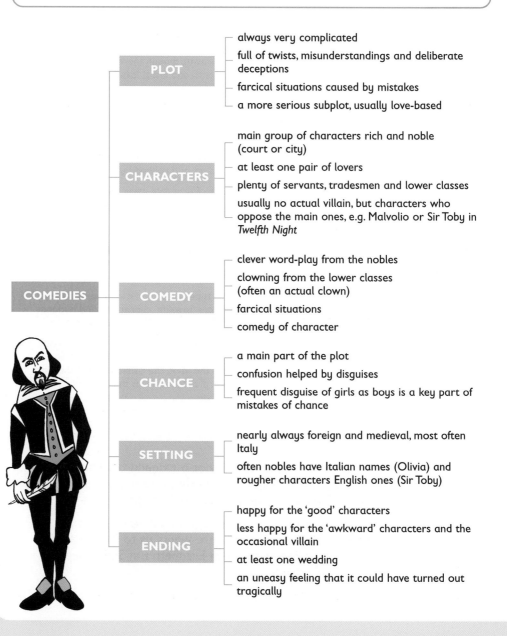

COMEDIES

PLOT
- always very complicated
- full of twists, misunderstandings and deliberate deceptions
- farcical situations caused by mistakes
- a more serious subplot, usually love-based

CHARACTERS
- main group of characters rich and noble (court or city)
- at least one pair of lovers
- plenty of servants, tradesmen and lower classes
- usually no actual villain, but characters who oppose the main ones, e.g. Malvolio or Sir Toby in *Twelfth Night*

COMEDY
- clever word-play from the nobles
- clowning from the lower classes (often an actual clown)
- farcical situations
- comedy of character

CHANCE
- a main part of the plot
- confusion helped by disguises
- frequent disguise of girls as boys is a key part of mistakes of chance

SETTING
- nearly always foreign and medieval, most often Italy
- often nobles have Italian names (Olivia) and rougher characters English ones (Sir Toby)

ENDING
- happy for the 'good' characters
- less happy for the 'awkward' characters and the occasional villain
- at least one wedding
- an uneasy feeling that it could have turned out tragically

Disguises, deceptions, misunderstandings: a typical plot!

THE TWINS IN *TWELFTH NIGHT*

Young twins, looking exactly like each other, except that one is male and the other female, take a sea journey. Their ship is wrecked.

Viola	Sebastian
is saved in Illyria and thinks her brother **Sebastian** is dead	survives and is sure that his sister **Viola** is dead
disguises herself as a boy by the name of **Cesario**	is rescued by Antonio, an enemy of Illyria

Cesario looks just like Sebastian.

Cesario (Viola) gets work at the court of Orsino. Orsino loves Countess Olivia.	Antonio helps **Sebastian** by giving him money. As a wanted man, Antonio must keep a low profile.
Viola (Cesario) falls in love with Orsino.	
Cesario (Viola) takes messages from Orsino to Olivia, who falls in love with him (her).	
Rivals for Olivia's love challenge **Cesario** to a duel. **Viola** is scared. Antonio arrives... and joins the fight. Soldiers arrive, see Antonio, arrest him. Antonio...	... sees **Sebastian** in trouble...
	... now needs his money back and asks **Sebastian** for it...
... but **Viola (Cesario)** refuses.	
Later **Cesario's** enemies attack...	... **Sebastian**, who beats them up!
Then Olivia asks **Cesario** to marry her...	... and **Sebastian** agrees!
Orsino is horrified that **Cesario** has been so ungrateful as to marry Olivia.	Antonio is horrified that **Sebastian** has been so ungrateful as to keep his money.

Eventually Viola and Sebastian recognise each other. Viola no longer needs her disguise.

Viola marries Orsino.	Orsino agrees to **Sebastian** marrying Olivia.

And this is just a sample of *Twelfth Night's* many deceptions and misunderstandings!

Keep on track

In your tests you concentrate on specific scenes in your Shakespeare play. When revising, make sure you know those scenes in great detail, but don't forget the rest of the play. You can't know what's important about a scene without knowing how it fits into the play as a whole.

Ask yourself questions like:

- Why does this character behave like this?
- How was this meeting set up?
- What will be the consequences of these events?

Try this!

Find out how many Shakespeare comedies are set in Italy. Some of the titles (but by no means all) give it away.

Reading

19

Shakespeare: tragedies

Why does this matter?

You will study at least two Shakespeare plays during Key Stage 3 and Key Stage 4. Probably one of these will be a tragedy. It is helpful:

- to know and recognise the form of a Shakespearean tragedy;

- to be familiar with the idea of the tragic hero – a noble character brought low by enemies, chance and his or her own failings.

What is prose?

Prose is ordinary writing or speech, not poetry. Your essays are written in prose; you speak prose.

✓ William Shakespeare (1564–1616) was the major playwright of the first great age of theatre in England in the reigns of Queen Elizabeth I and King James I.

✓ The plays of Shakespeare (and most of the other writers of the time) are divided into tragedies, comedies and histories.

✓ Well-known tragedies by Shakespeare include such plays as *Othello*, *Hamlet* and *King Lear*.

✓ The tragedies you are most likely to study are *Macbeth* and *Romeo and Juliet*.

TRAGEDIES

PLOT
- story of a successful (noble?) person
- from greatness to disaster and (usually) death
- downfall helped by weakness and mistakes

CHARACTERS
- main character (protagonist) as tragic hero
- two main characters in love tragedies like *Romeo and Juliet*
- usually a villain (e.g. Iago in *Othello*) to help destroy the protagonist
- Macbeth is his own villain – or is it the Witches?
- wide range of supporting characters: nobles, friends, servants

COMEDY
- main plot tragic, with sombre ending, but...
- clown figures often add humour (e.g. Porter in *Macbeth*)
- foolish or witty nobles (e.g. Mercutio) create comedy
- even some protagonists (e.g. Hamlet) have comic scenes

CHANCE
- tragedy not only caused by villainy and weakness
- coincidence or bad luck plays a part, e.g. the timing of Romeo and Juliet's marriage and Tybalt's death

SETTING
- never England in Shakespeare's own time
- usually somewhere remote in time, e.g. eleventh-century Scotland
- somewhere small enough for a personal power struggle, e.g. Verona in the Middle Ages

ENDING
- the death of the main character(s)
- often their enemies die, too
- order is then restored: Malcolm becomes King (*Macbeth*) or the warring families make peace (*Romeo and Juliet*)

What is a soliloquy?

'Soliloquy' comes from two Latin words meaning 'alone-speak'. A main character, alone on the stage, tells us what he or she really thinks.

> If it were done when 'tis done, then 'twere well
> It were done quickly: if th'assassination
> Could trammel up the consequence and catch
> With his surcease, success...

Macbeth speaks of murdering the King and his wish that it could all be over quickly; he goes on to talk of his fear of punishment. He dare not tell the other lords what he plans and Lady Macbeth would mock his fears, but he can tell the audience, and we know he is speaking the truth.

Blank verse, prose or rhyme?

BLANK VERSE (unrhymed)
- noble character speaking seriously
- speaking of love or war or kingship or political power, e.g. Romeo and Juliet (love) or Macduff and Malcolm (the Crown)
- most soliloquies
- occasionally a lower-class character on a tragic subject, e.g. Nurse on Tybalt's death

PROSE
- upper-class joking
- nobles dealing with lower classes (often, not always)
- lower class or comic characters, e.g. Nurse or Porter

RHYME
- love poems: sonnets and couplets, e.g. Romeo and Juliet
- songs and charms, e.g. Witches
- some couplets to round off a scene or make a strong point:
    Strange things I have in head, that will to hand,
    Which must be acted, ere they may be scanned.
    (*Macbeth,* Act 3, Scene 4)

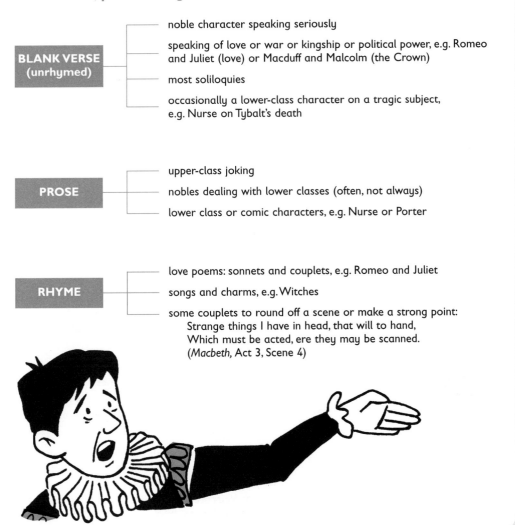

Keep on track

Learning quotations is very important in Shakespeare – or, if you are allowed the text in your tests, learning where to find important quotations.

- Use short quotations: two words or two lines, perhaps, not ten lines.
- Learn them complete: don't break off mid-phrase.
- Make sure you know exactly what they mean: quotations must be relevant.

Try this!

There are three love tragedies by Shakespeare named after both lovers and at least eight other tragedies. See if you can find out the names of all the tragedies.

Reading

21

Why does this matter?

Most of Shakespeare's history plays are part of a sequence covering 1398 to 1485. It is perfectly possible to enjoy and understand *Henry V* on its own, but it helps to be aware of the past. For example, Henry V prays before battle:

'Not today, O Lord, O, not today, think not upon the fault My father made in compassing the crown!'

And is it true?

Mostly yes, but the *Henry IV* plays and *Henry V* are full of invented characters, notably Falstaff, his companions and Mistress Quickly and (in *Henry V*) the various captains and soldiers.

✓ William Shakespeare (1564–1616) was the major playwright of the first great age of theatre in England in the reigns of Queen Elizabeth I and King James I.

✓ The plays of Shakespeare (and most of the other writers of the time) are divided into tragedies, comedies and histories.

✓ The history plays deal with English history of the twelfth to sixteenth centuries, each one named after a king of England.

✓ The history play you are most likely to study is *Henry V*.

HISTORIES

PLOT
- dictated by events of the period
- some kind of power struggle, usually for the throne
- often a mixture of great events and more trivial incidents
- major events reasonably accurate historically
- more trivial matters invented by Shakespeare

CHARACTERS
- the King is always central
- he may be presented as heroic (Henry V) or evil (Richard III) or anything in between
- rebels of varying importance (the Percies are the most striking)
- many lords, some individual characters, some mere background
- 'low-life' characters (invented by Shakespeare) very prominent in later plays

COMEDY
- some plays (like *Richard II*) lack comedy
- in different ways there is humour in kings Richard III and Henry V
- main comedy from 'low-life' characters, notably Falstaff and companions in the *Henry IV* plays; the companions reappear in *Henry V*

CHANCE
- chance plays less part than in tragedies and comedies
- the story is known – this gives certainty
- those who overthrow kings are guilty and certain to be punished

SETTING
- England, mostly between the end of the fourteenth and the end of the fifteenth centuries
- some events elsewhere, notably France in *Henry V*
- the Royal Court, castles and palaces, taverns, lodging-houses, roadsides and battlefields

ENDING
- many end with the overthrow of an unsuccessful king
- *Henry V*, about a very successful king, ends with news of his death and the disasters that follow
- several plays are in series (Part 1, etc.), so end looking forward to the next part

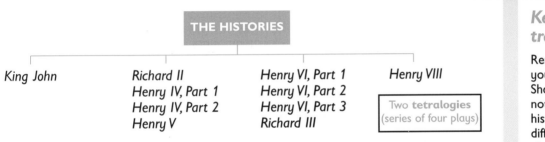

THE HISTORIES

| King John | Richard II
Henry IV, Part 1
Henry IV, Part 2
Henry V | Henry VI, Part 1
Henry VI, Part 2
Henry VI, Part 3
Richard III | Henry VIII |

Two **tetralogies**
(series of four plays)

From Richard II to Henry V

The history

Richard II, King of England
(1377–1399)
Overthrown after a long reign by his cousin Henry Bolingbroke (whom he had banished) and the Percies, a great northern family, Richard was murdered in 1400.

Henry IV, King of England
(1399–1413)
His reign was troubled by rebellions by the Percies and the Welsh and by illness. In later years there was an attempt to force his abdication in favour of his son.

Henry V, King of England
(1413–1422)
He spent most of his reign fighting in support of his claim to the French crown. Great success (Agincourt, 1415), married a French princess, but died young, leaving his infant son as Henry VI.

The plays

Richard II deals only with the last year of Richard's reign. Bolingbroke is banished, returns to claim his lands when his father dies and overthrows Richard to become Henry IV.

Henry IV, Part 1, is all based on the Percy rebellion and reaches a climax at the Battle of Shrewsbury (1403). Shakespeare's additions include the Prince of Wales' wildness and invented companions like Falstaff.

Part 2 is set much later in the reign: there is rivalry between father and son and the king feels great guilt for Richard II's death. He dies in Act 4 and the Prince becomes Henry V.

Henry V deals entirely with preparing for the French war, success in battle and wooing the Princess. The king is worried that his father's guilt might be passed on to him and an Epilogue tells of his death and the troubled reign of Henry VI, the subject of the next series of plays.

Keep on track

Remember, what you are studying is Shakespeare's play, not history. The history plays are different from other plays (like *King Lear*, set in Ancient Britain, which doesn't pretend to be accurate) in claiming to be truthful. Knowing the history helps, but what really matters is Shakespeare's version.

So, in *Henry V* Fluellen (who never existed) is as real as the Duke of Exeter (who did).

And is it true?

Most of the events are, though many years of the reigns are left out, but what about the characters? Shakespeare began writing in Queen Elizabeth's reign and he accepts the official Elizabethan view. In particular, her grandfather, Henry VII, over-threw Richard III, so Richard III is presented as evil.

Reading

Why does this matter?

- Reading Shakespeare aloud is much easier if you are aware of the rhythm of the verse.

- At the same time, verse should not be read in a special 'poetry voice': people can be angry, confused or unbalanced in verse as well as being noble, romantic or heroic.

- Shakespeare limits his use of rhyme. It helps to know where he uses it.

It's not just Shakespeare

Don't think that this use of verse is an oddity of Shakespeare's. It was normal for Elizabethan playwrights. In fact, some earlier ones used rhyming couplets all the time – which you would find very artificial.

Reading

✓ Shakespeare's plays contain large amounts of verse.

✓ Most serious speeches by noble characters are in verse.

✓ Most Shakespearean verse (not all) is blank verse.

✓ Blank verse does not rhyme, but has lines of regular length.

Blank verse 1: Formal speech

Twelfth Night: Olivia explains why she cannot marry Orsino (Act 1, Scene 5).

Blank verse
Five stresses in a line, normally 10 syllables.

> Your lord does know my mind; I cannot love him.
> Yet I suppose him virtuous, know him noble,
> Of gréat estáte, of frésh and stáinless yóuth;
> In voices well divulged, free, learned and valiant,
> And in dimension and the shape of nature
> A grácious pérson. But yét I cánnot lóve him.

Each stressed syllable marked with ´.

Shakespeare didn't worry about counting syllables. You'll find 12 in the last line – but there are still only five stresses.

Rhyme 1: Song and dance

Twelfth Night: Feste the jester sings (Act 2, Scene 4).

Repeated phrases
You often find those in songs – think of pop songs.

> **Come away, come away,** death,
>   And in sad cypress let me be laid.
> **Fly away, fly away,** breath;
>   I am slain by a fair cruel maid.
> My shroud of white, stuck all with yew,
>   O, prepare it.
> My part of death, no one so true
>   Did share it.

A sad song, but pretty, not agonized.

Note the different line lengths, which give you the pattern of the tune.

What's the difference?

Macbeth: The Witches (Act 4, Scene 1)

The words are menacing – what of the verse?

> **Fillet of a fenny snake**
> In the cauldron boil and bake;
> **Eye of newt,** and **toe of frog**
> **Wool of bat** and **tongue of dog**

The short rhyming lines are a chant, not a song, and build tension.

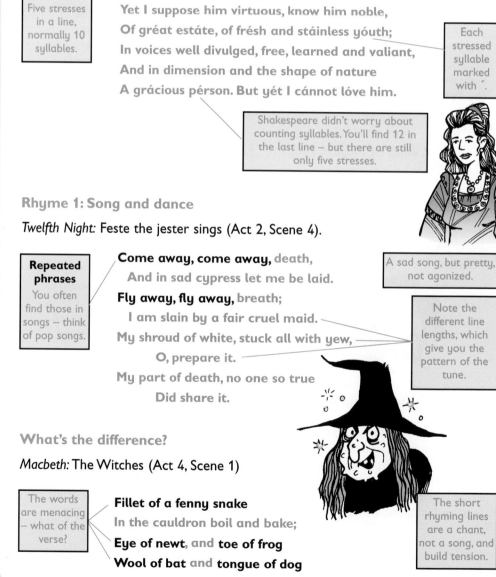

Blank verse 2: Fury and distraction

Macbeth is preparing for battle (Act 5, Scene 3). He is speaking to the Doctor and his servant Seyton.

> Throw physic to the dogs, I'll none of it.
> Come, put mine armour on; give me my staff –
> Seyton, send out. – Doctor, the thanes fly from me. –
> Come, sir, dispatch. – If you couldst, doctor, cast
> The water of my land, find her disease,
> And purge it to a sound and pristine health,
> I would applaud thee to the very echo
> That should applaud again. – Pull't off, I say.

'Verse' doesn't always mean poetic language.

Although this is verse, it's very jerky and abrupt. Macbeth cannot concentrate and turns from the Doctor to Seyton and back again.

Rhyme 2: Romantic speech

Twelfth Night: Olivia confesses her love for Cesario (Act 3, Scene 1).

These two couplets are part of a series of nine on the subject of love and devotion.

> Cesario, by the roses of the Spring,
> By maidhood, honour, truth and everything,
> I love thee so that, maugre all thy pride,
> Nor wit nor wisdom can my passion hide.

In *Romeo and Juliet* Shakespeare even gives the lovers sonnets (14-line love poems) to speak to each other.

Rhyme 3: Emphasis

Henry V: The King sets off to make war against France. These last lines of Act 2, Scene 2 come at the end of a long speech in blank verse.

The couplet emphasises what he is going to do.

> Let us deliver
> Our puissance into the hand of God,
> Putting it straight in expedition.
> **Cheerly to sea; the signs of war advance:**
> **No king of England, if not king of France.**

In *Henry V* Shakespeare frequently ends a scene with a couplet, as though saying, 'This is the important message of this scene.'

Keep on track

Timing is all-important in any test or examination. You shouldn't finish too early: that means that you probably have not included enough information. However, you must make sure that you finish, otherwise you lose marks. Find out from your teacher just how long you have and maybe write a practice answer against the clock.

Do you know…?

When does Shakespeare use verse and when does he use prose? If you are not sure, check the entry in **Shakespeare: tragedies** (page 21).

Reading

Why does this matter?

- A poet's meaning (or a poetic playwright's – like Shakespeare) is partly contained in the comparisons he or she makes. William Blake would not have written about a lamb being forged in a factory!

- Always think of interesting ways to improve your own writing: look for imaginative comparisons and avoid dead metaphors.

Use your imagination!

Many words began life as metaphors. 'Skyscraper' was originally an exaggerated comparison; now it's the correct term. The same applies to the 'beefeaters' at the Tower of London. How many more can you think of?

✓ If you state actual fact, that is the literal truth.

✓ In your writing, you can often use comparisons to explain things more clearly or vividly.

✓ A simile is an open comparison, usually with 'like' or 'as'.

✓ A metaphor is a hidden comparison (when you use the comparison instead of the literal truth).

SIMILES

- are used constantly in speech and writing
- are often so familiar that they add nothing to your writing: e.g. 'as good as gold' or 'like lightning'
- usually use 'like' or 'as', but 'brighter than the sun' is also a simile
- must fit the reason for comparison: size, speed, colour, age, etc.
- need to make the right appeal to the reader as well: e.g. 'He had teeth like a crocodile's' compares tooth size, but with an extra hint of menace – you would only use it of a favourite uncle if you wanted contrast.

METAPHORS

- are just as common as similes
- may be used too often to be of any use, becoming 'dead metaphors': e.g. 'raining cats and dogs' or 'keep your nose to the grindstone'
- can involve referring to someone/something as something different: e.g. 'He was a tiger when roused' or 'the queen of the catwalk'
- often consist of someone/something's actions being described in terms of something different: e.g. 'The team stormed upfield', 'The troops butchered their enemies' or 'The breeze whispered in the trees'
- these metaphors are perfectly usable, but best of all is to invent your own
- avoid mixed metaphors except as a joke: e.g. 'She sailed into town, paid us a flying visit, then steamed into the distance.'

Reading

PERSONIFICATION
- a form of metaphor
- is used when something not alive is described in personal terms: e.g. names like 'Old Father Thames' or 'Britannia'
- more often the actions of things are described as if they are people: e.g. 'The sky wept to see her grief' or 'The house invited us to come in'

RECURRENT METAPHORS
- often a poet will use similar metaphors several times; this is to link the ideas and feelings of the poem together
- Shakespeare uses recurrent metaphors frequently: think of the Macbeths and all the metaphors of blood
- read the lines below for a good example of recurrent metaphor

A recurrent metaphor in poetry

In the poem 'The Tyger' William Blake asks the question, 'What made the tyger?'. Later in the poem he asks the question again in these terms:

What the *hammer*? What the *chain*?
In what *furnace* was thy brain?
What the *anvil*? What dread grasp
Dare its deadly terrors clasp?

When Blake was writing, the development of factories was new and rather frightening. He writes as though the terrifying tiger was built out of metal in a factory.

Keep on track

Sometimes you have to learn things by heart by repeating a list until it sticks in your memory. If possible, though, avoid that by making connections between pieces of information you have to remember so that thinking of one triggers off the other(s).

Always aim for understanding rather than simply memorising.

Shakespeare's metaphors

One of these should be familiar to you: 'star-crossed lovers' (*Romeo and Juliet*), 'this dead butcher' (*Macbeth*), 'assume the port of Mars' (*Henry V*) or the first line of *Twelfth Night*, 'If music be the food of love…'.

Reading

- We all see newspapers and most of us read them. We need to think about how they work and how they influence us.

- The study of media is now a set part of the English course in schools. 'Media' simply means methods of passing on information and views – and one of the main methods is via newspapers.

Share the joke!

Tabloid headlines are well known for using jokes and puns. What do you think the headlines 'Tyke that, cowboy!' and 'Eeh Bah Gun!' in the *Daily Star* referred to? (Check your answer on the next page.)

Reading

✓ To be successful, newspapers have to aim at a particular type of reader. In this way they not only build up sales, but appeal to advertisers who know the reading public they are reaching.

✓ National newspapers can be divided into two types: broadsheets and tabloids. This refers to their size (a tabloid page size is half as big as a broadsheet), but also reflects their approach to news.

BROADSHEETS

- *The Times, Guardian, Daily Telegraph, Independent*
- main headline on front page usually 'serious' news
- usually about four or five stories on front page
- headlines vary in size, but big bold capitals are rare
- main picture (colour) usually no more than a quarter of front page
- often a separate review section on arts, lifestyle, political comment etc.
- 'human interest' stories covered, but usually not prominently
- pages of financial news and lists of investments
- good sports coverage
- ordinary daily size over 40 large pages

TABLOIDS

- *Daily Mail, Express, Sun, Mirror, Star*
- main headline may be serious news, but it's often an 'exclusive' story about a showbusiness or sports star
- usually one main story on front page and probably one other
- headlines in bold capitals: a six-word headline can fill over a quarter of the front page
- main picture (colour) can take well over half front page
- detailed television listings, but little by way of arts reviews
- political comment largely to do with personalities
- 'human interest' stories (often about celebrities) are prominent
- varying amounts of financial news, but not page after page of lists
- good sports coverage, with stronger personal opinion
- ordinary daily size over 40 smaller pages

Remember:

- These are generalisations and cannot be true in every case.
- In particular, you may be looking at an 80-page *Daily Mail* with a large section on finance and several pages of film, book and theatre reviews.

Take a look at how newspapers influence their readers...

MAKING NEWS

- tabloids frequently create their own stories: 'Fans turn on Goal King Al' (*Mirror*, 6.6.00) – the main sports story is the result of the paper's own poll
- see how many 'exclusive' interviews are front page news
- the choice of people interviewed tells us what the paper thinks is important

PLACING NEWS

- a straight news story (for example, a non-fatal rail crash) may be dealt with in similar words by all papers
- the editor's attitude is shown by where it is placed in the paper: second story on the front page (with picture) or seven paragraphs on page 8?
- inside the paper, right-hand pages tend to get the reader's attention: see what different newspapers place there (especially pages 3 and 5)

CAMPAIGNING

- tabloids frequently try to influence public opinion: in politics (especially during elections) they support one party
- during Euro 2000 many tabloids opposed the choice of stadium for England v. Germany: 'Stop this folly' (*Mail*) and 'Switch it now!' (*Mirror*) are not news headlines, but expressions of opinion.

CREATING PERSONALITIES

- look at the way in which different papers treat 'personalities', e.g. politicians, sports stars, television stars, the royal family
- to encourage us to admire, fear, love or ridicule these people they use techniques which include nicknames, cartoons, photographs, readers' polls, interviews etc.

Keep on track

Do you ever get a chance to compare different newspapers? Maybe you have a paper round or the school library takes more than one daily paper. Compare their different approaches:

- Do they want us to support the Government?
- Are they campaigning against the England football manager?
- Do they want us to think the Millennium Dome is a waste of time and money?

Did you work it out?

The headlines in **Share the joke!** referred to a story that a Yorkshireman, Ben Thompson, was one of the most feared gunslingers in the Wild West!

Reading

Nouns

Why does this matter?

Nouns and verbs are the two basic parts of speech. To put together sentences you need to use both correctly. (Look at **Sentences**, pages 42–43.) It's very important that you can identify nouns and verbs almost without thinking about it – you can work out everything else from there.

Know the difference – common and proper

- Using capital letters properly depends on knowing the difference between common and proper nouns.

- Good use of proper nouns can make your writing more personal and involve the readers more. Too much use without explanation can confuse them.

✓ A noun is frequently described as a naming word. This is a simple, but fairly accurate, description. However, nouns are often not 'names' in the usual sense.

✓ Nouns can be referred to as common (the general name) or proper (an individual name). You need to understand the difference.

✓ The name for a group of individuals is known as a collective noun.

✓ Pronouns can often be used to take the place of nouns: e.g. 'man' (common noun) can be replaced by the pronoun 'he' or 'him'.

Common
The general name of a type of person/animal/place/object, not an individual: 'girl', 'cat', 'city', 'medal'.

NOUNS

Proper
The name of an individual: 'Charlotte', 'Macavity', 'Manchester', 'Victoria Cross'.

Collective
The name given to a single group made up of many different individuals: 'herd', 'class', 'team'.

Don't forget that **collective nouns are singular:** they count as one. There is only one team or pack or pile, though there are many players or wolves or boxes: 'The pupils were badly behaved', but 'The class was badly behaved'.

- Capital letters: all proper nouns begin with a capital letter. Common nouns don't begin with a capital, unless there is some other reason, like the start of a sentence:
'My friend Jack lives in a village near Norwich.'

- Common nouns become proper nouns when they are part of a title:
'She was going to school' and 'He was playing in the park' but 'She went to Park High School'.

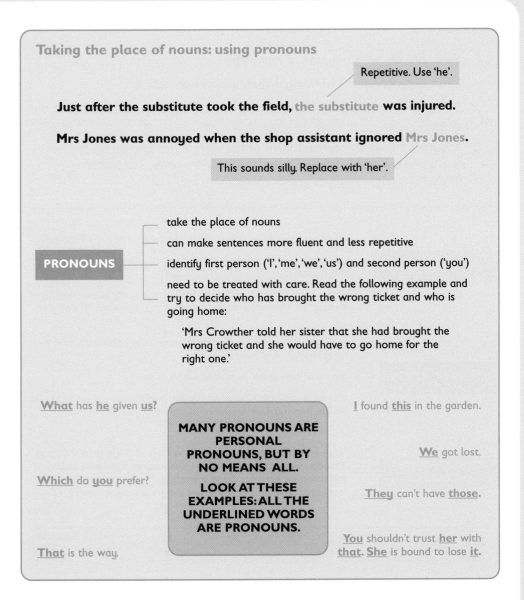

Taking the place of nouns: using pronouns

Repetitive. Use 'he'.

Just after the substitute took the field, the substitute was injured.

Mrs Jones was annoyed when the shop assistant ignored Mrs Jones.

This sounds silly. Replace with 'her'.

PRONOUNS
- take the place of nouns
- can make sentences more fluent and less repetitive
- identify first person ('I', 'me', 'we', 'us') and second person ('you')
- need to be treated with care. Read the following example and try to decide who has brought the wrong ticket and who is going home:

'Mrs Crowther told her sister that she had brought the wrong ticket and she would have to go home for the right one.'

<u>What</u> has <u>he</u> given <u>us</u>?

<u>I</u> found <u>this</u> in the garden.

MANY PRONOUNS ARE PERSONAL PRONOUNS, BUT BY NO MEANS ALL.

LOOK AT THESE EXAMPLES: ALL THE UNDERLINED WORDS ARE PRONOUNS.

<u>We</u> got lost.

<u>Which</u> do <u>you</u> prefer?

<u>They</u> can't have <u>those</u>.

<u>That</u> is the way.

<u>You</u> shouldn't trust <u>her</u> with <u>that</u>. <u>She</u> is bound to lose <u>it</u>.

Abstract and concrete

You can also divide nouns into abstract and concrete. This is not an easy idea to grasp, but it is useful to know.

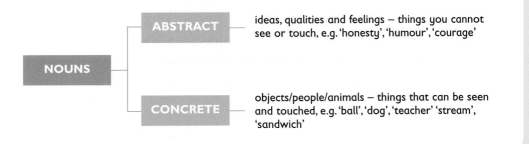

NOUNS

ABSTRACT — ideas, qualities and feelings – things you cannot see or touch, e.g. 'honesty', 'humour', 'courage'

CONCRETE — objects/people/animals – things that can be seen and touched, e.g. 'ball', 'dog', 'teacher' 'stream', 'sandwich'

Keep on track

Knowing about nouns is essential, but it's a matter of understanding more than learning facts. Make out a chart with three columns, 'common', 'proper' and 'collective', and fill them with nouns that match each other: e.g. 'footballer' (common), 'Tony Adams' (proper), 'team' (collective), or 'singer' (common), 'Victoria Adams' (proper) and 'band' (collective).

Try this!

Here's a start for your revision exercise. Put these words in the right columns (common, proper or collective), one word per row, then complete the row with matching words:

teacher, flock, Tony Blair, gang, Harry Potter, soldier.

Writing

Why does this matter?

The subject and verb are the key parts of a sentence (see **Sentences**, pages 42–43). It is important to remove the common errors in the use of verbs from your writing. If you find it easier to learn from examples than from words like participles and agreement, then do so, but make sure that you use the different forms of the verb correctly.

Find the irregulars!

Most verbs keep the same basic form through the various tenses: e.g. 'rise', 'rises', 'rising', 'rose', 'risen'. The different parts of the verb 'to be' are nothing like each other: 'am', 'is', 'are', 'being', 'was', 'were', 'been'. See if you can think of any other verbs that are irregular in this way.

✓ Verbs are an essential part of language.

✓ Most verbs are verbs of doing – they express an action.

✓ Some verbs are verbs of being – they help to tell us something about the subject.

✓ You need to use the correct form of the verb depending on tense (past, present or future) and number (singular – one – or plural – more than one).

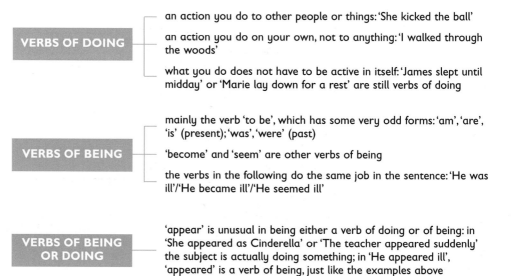

VERBS OF DOING
- an action you do to other people or things: 'She kicked the ball'
- an action you do on your own, not to anything: 'I walked through the woods'
- what you do does not have to be active in itself: 'James slept until midday' or 'Marie lay down for a rest' are still verbs of doing

VERBS OF BEING
- mainly the verb 'to be', which has some very odd forms: 'am', 'are', 'is' (present); 'was', 'were' (past)
- 'become' and 'seem' are other verbs of being
- the verbs in the following do the same job in the sentence: 'He was ill'/'He became ill'/'He seemed ill'

VERBS OF BEING OR DOING
- 'appear' is unusual in being either a verb of doing or of being: in 'She appeared as Cinderella' or 'The teacher appeared suddenly' the subject is actually doing something; in 'He appeared ill', 'appeared' is a verb of being, just like the examples above

'Lie', 'lay', 'laid', 'lied'

Perhaps the most confusing set of verbs is based on the word 'lie':

- 'lie' (past tense 'lay') means to be flat or horizontal or in a certain place: 'The fields lie behind the school.'/'This morning he lay in bed until 11 o'clock.'/'The dog was lying by the fire.'

- 'lay' (past tense 'laid') is to put something down: 'Will you lay those books next to mine?'/'The Queen laid a wreath at the Cenotaph.'/'The council is laying a new road surface.'

- 'lie' (past tense 'lied') means to tell an untruth: 'He lied to me.' In the other tenses it takes the same form as the other 'lie'.

AGREEMENT

- different parts of your sentence/paragraph should match each other
- if you are writing in the past tense, don't change to the present without a reason (or from present to past)
- make sure that your subject and verb agree on number: 'the teachers' is plural and must be followed by 'were' (plural), not 'was' (singular)
- in some areas 'we was', 'she were' etc. are common in speech; they are never correct in writing

PAST PARTICIPLE

- a part of the word that is used with 'to be' or 'to have' to make up different tenses: e.g. 'It is finished' or 'Mr Green has left the register behind'
- often it is the same as the past tense: e.g. 'finished' and 'left'
- where it is different, you must take care to use the right form: 'Humpty Dumpty has fallen' (not 'fell'), 'It is written down here' (not 'wrote'), 'My father has gone to the station' (not 'went'), 'The key is frozen in the lock' (not 'froze')

PRESENT PARTICIPLE

- the '-ing' form of the verb
- used with 'to be' to show something going on continuously: 'The Head is still keeping them behind' or 'The football squad was practising after school' (note that despite its name it can be used in the past)
- be careful to use the present, not the past, participle for ongoing things the subject is/was/will be doing: e.g. 'The landlord is standing by the door' (not 'stood'), 'My friend is sitting in front of me' (not 'sat')

Keep on track

Revision can be boring. Don't let it reach that stage by planning your time to build in variety: Science is always more interesting if it provides a break from English!

Verb or adjective?

Participles can also be used as adjectives to describe nouns: 'the spent cartridge', 'the falling building', 'a defeated challenger', 'a promising footballer'.

Writing

Why does this matter?

An accurate and imaginative use of adjectives and adverbs is essential to good writing. You should beware of:

• confusing adjectives and adverbs

• using the same adjective (e.g. 'great' or 'nice' or 'scary') too often

• exaggerated and slangy use of adjectives like 'fabulous' or 'tremendous'

Listen to the radio

How often have you heard a football manager say, 'We did <u>good</u> after half-time' or 'We came out too <u>slow</u>'?

Under no circumstances should you do the same, even if you support his team!

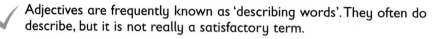

✓ Adjectives are frequently known as 'describing words'. They often do describe, but it is not really a satisfactory term.

✓ **Adjectives** tell us more about **nouns** or **pronouns**, sometimes by describing them.

✓ **Adverbs** tell us more about **verbs**.

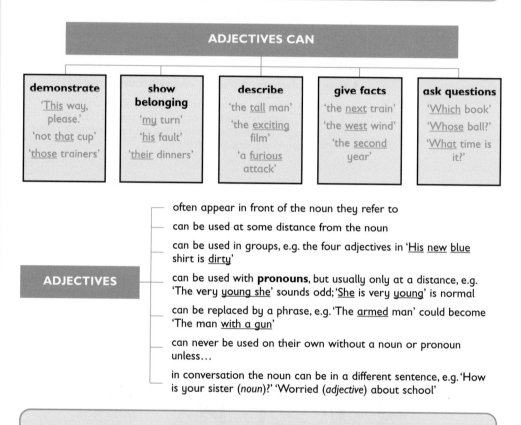

ADJECTIVES CAN

demonstrate	show belonging	describe	give facts	ask questions
'This way, please.'	'my turn'	'the tall man'	'the next train'	'Which book'
'not that cup'	'his fault'	'the exciting film'	'the west wind'	'Whose ball?'
'those trainers'	'their dinners'	'a furious attack'	'the second year'	'What time is it?'

ADJECTIVES

— often appear in front of the noun they refer to

— can be used at some distance from the noun

— can be used in groups, e.g. the four adjectives in 'His new blue shirt is dirty'

— can be used with **pronouns**, but usually only at a distance, e.g. 'The very young she' sounds odd; 'She is very young' is normal

— can be replaced by a phrase, e.g. 'The armed man' could become 'The man with a gun'

— can never be used on their own without a noun or pronoun unless…

— in conversation the noun can be in a different sentence, e.g. 'How is your sister (noun)?' 'Worried (adjective) about school'

Comparatives

Adjectives can also compare two, or more than two, things or people:

• 'He is <u>tall</u>' – 'He is <u>taller</u> than his father' (comparing two) – 'He is <u>tallest</u> of all' (comparing more than two)

• Usually use '-er' and '-est' for short words ('bright', 'brighter', 'brightest'), 'more' and 'most' for long words ('intelligent', 'more intelligent', 'most intelligent')

• Beware some odd forms: what happens to 'good' and 'bad'?

• Remember to use '-er' if comparing two: 'City was the <u>better</u> (not 'best') team today.'

Adjectives

tell us about a **noun** (a person or thing)

'The <u>slow</u> train'
The train (*noun*) is described as slow because it is always like that.

'<u>Fierce</u> creatures'
The creatures are fierce; it is in their nature.

'This is a <u>good</u> book.'
The book as a whole is something you admire; it is in general good.

Adverbs

tell us about a **verb** (an action)

'The train moves <u>slowly</u>'
At this time it moves (*verb*) slowly; it may not be a slow train normally.

'Martina volleyed <u>fiercely</u>.'
This action, the shot, was done fiercely; it says nothing about Martina's character.

'He brings out the humour <u>well</u>.'
You are praising how the author does one thing. The book may be poor in many ways, but he does this well.

Note

• Most adverbs are formed by adding '-ly' to the adjective. You will see that 'good' is an exception.

• Some adjectives end in '-ly': 'lively' (*adjective*)/'livelily' (*adverb*).

What is the difference?

Many descriptive adjectives have similar meanings, but suggest different feelings.

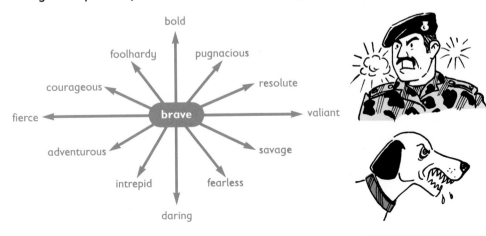

bold
foolhardy   pugnacious
courageous   resolute
fierce   **brave**   valiant
adventurous   savage
intrepid   fearless
daring

Keep on track

There are very few parts of speech that you must know for an English examination, but you must know those without hesitation or doubt. A word like conjunction is useful to know, but, so long as you understand the importance of joining words, it is not essential. The same applies to preposition.

The five you must know are noun, pronoun, verb, adjective and adverb. Learn them now, write down their meanings and check them when you revise.

Try this!

Look at the ring of adjectives around 'brave'.

See if you can make similar circles of words with similar meanings, but different feelings and effects, for:
    quiet
    thin
    soft
    strong

Writing

Prefixes and suffixes

Why does this matter?

- Prefixes (and to some extent suffixes) are one of the main aids to working out the meaning of words you have never seen before. They give you the meaning of at least one part of the word.

- Prefixes help to form many new words: you can even use them to make words for yourself. Anyone could work out what 'anti-homework' or 'trans-school' or 'pre-revision' means.

The longest word?

It is claimed that 'antidisestablish-mentarianism' is the longest word in the dictionary. Try breaking it into sections and see if you have any idea of its meaning.

Writing

✓ A prefix is a syllable or several syllables which can be added to the front of a word.

✓ A suffix is a syllable or several syllables added to the end of a word.

✓ Both prefixes and suffixes have a constant meaning (or, occasionally, more than one meaning) whatever word they are attached to.

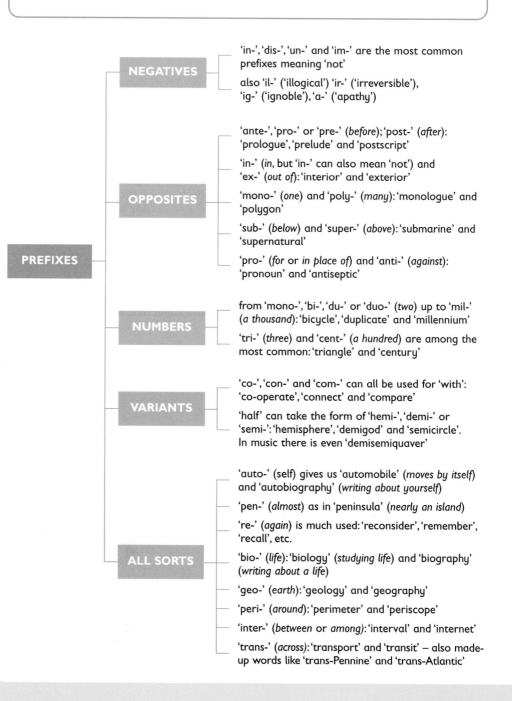

NEGATIVES
- 'in-', 'dis-', 'un-' and 'im-' are the most common prefixes meaning 'not'
- also 'il-' ('illogical') 'ir-' ('irreversible'), 'ig-' ('ignoble'), 'a-' ('apathy')

OPPOSITES
- 'ante-', 'pro-' or 'pre-' (*before*); 'post-' (*after*): 'prologue', 'prelude' and 'postscript'
- 'in-' (*in*, but 'in-' can also mean 'not') and 'ex-' (*out of*): 'interior' and 'exterior'
- 'mono-' (*one*) and 'poly-' (*many*): 'monologue' and 'polygon'
- 'sub-' (*below*) and 'super-' (*above*): 'submarine' and 'supernatural'
- 'pro-' (*for or in place of*) and 'anti-' (*against*): 'pronoun' and 'antiseptic'

NUMBERS
- from 'mono-', 'bi-', 'du-' or 'duo-' (*two*) up to 'mil-' (*a thousand*): 'bicycle', 'duplicate' and 'millennium'
- 'tri-' (*three*) and 'cent-' (*a hundred*) are among the most common: 'triangle' and 'century'

VARIANTS
- 'co-', 'con-' and 'com-' can all be used for 'with': 'co-operate', 'connect' and 'compare'
- 'half' can take the form of 'hemi-', 'demi-' or 'semi-': 'hemisphere', 'demigod' and 'semicircle'. In music there is even 'demisemiquaver'

ALL SORTS
- 'auto-' (*self*) gives us 'automobile' (*moves by itself*) and 'autobiography' (*writing about yourself*)
- 'pen-' (*almost*) as in 'peninsula' (*nearly an island*)
- 're-' (*again*) is much used: 'reconsider', 'remember', 'recall', etc.
- 'bio-' (*life*): 'biology' (*studying life*) and 'biography' (*writing about a life*)
- 'geo-' (*earth*): 'geology' and 'geography'
- 'peri-' (*around*): 'perimeter' and 'periscope'
- 'inter-' (*between or among*): 'interval' and 'internet'
- 'trans-' (*across*): 'transport' and 'transit' – also made-up words like 'trans-Pennine' and 'trans-Atlantic'

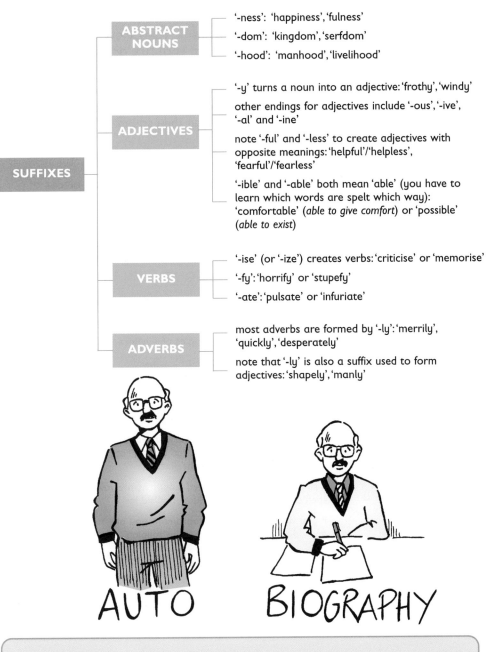

SUFFIXES

ABSTRACT NOUNS
- '-ness': 'happiness', 'fulness'
- '-dom': 'kingdom', 'serfdom'
- '-hood': 'manhood', 'livelihood'

ADJECTIVES
- '-y' turns a noun into an adjective: 'frothy', 'windy'
- other endings for adjectives include '-ous', '-ive', '-al' and '-ine'
- note '-ful' and '-less' to create adjectives with opposite meanings: 'helpful'/'helpless', 'fearful'/'fearless'
- '-ible' and '-able' both mean 'able' (you have to learn which words are spelt which way): 'comfortable' (*able to give comfort*) or 'possible' (*able to exist*)

VERBS
- '-ise' (or '-ize') creates verbs: 'criticise' or 'memorise'
- '-fy': 'horrify' or 'stupefy'
- '-ate': 'pulsate' or 'infuriate'

ADVERBS
- most adverbs are formed by '-ly': 'merrily', 'quickly', 'desperately'
- note that '-ly' is also a suffix used to form adjectives: 'shapely', 'manly'

AUTO BIOGRAPHY

Keep on track

Learning lists of things is not usually particularly helpful in English. Prefixes are an exception to this.

- Try to find examples in the dictionary.
- Just learn as many at a time as you can absorb.
- Be ready to apply your knowledge intelligently when you come across a new word.

A prefix or not?

You will have recognised that 'prefix' begins with the prefix 'pre-' (*before*). What about 'suffix'? 'Suf-' is a version of 'sub-' (*below*), so the suffix is the part that goes under the rest.

Making words

You can break a word into its separate parts and work out its meaning.

'Antepenultimate' = 'ante-' (before) + 'pen-' (almost) + 'ultimate' (last). It is the thing before the almost last: the last but two.

'Autobiography' = 'auto-' (self) + 'bio-' (life) + 'graphy' (writing). It is oneself writing about life: someone's own life story.

Writing

Spelling

Why does this matter?

- In all tests and examinations there is some method of reducing marks for poor spelling, whether it is an 'out of ten' approach for errors or a general impression.

- Writing is about communicating. Poor spelling causes poor communication and confuses readers.

Be in the top 8 per cent!

A survey in 1999 showed that the most commonly misspelt words are:
accommodate
disastrous
humorous
millennium
mischievous
pronunciation
privilege
separate
surprise
weird.

Only 8 per cent of 16–24-year-olds could spell them all.

Writing

✓ It is wrong to say that English spelling has no rules. However, it has few general rules, so you usually have to learn each rule or example separately.

✓ The way you spell and the way you speak are linked: sounding out new words will often help. But remember that there are many exceptions – words which are spelt nothing like the way they sound.

This is not a complete guide to English spelling, just some separate pieces of helpful guidance.

'I' BEFORE 'E' EXCEPT AFTER 'C'
- the full rule is **'i' before 'e' except after 'c' when the sound is 'ee'**; in this form it works well and is very useful
- 'ceiling' – 'e' before 'i' after 'c'
- 'either' – 'e' before 'i' is often pronounced 'eye'
- 'feign' or 'their' – 'e' before 'i' and the sound is 'ay'
- 'siege', 'fierce', 'field' – examples of 'i' before 'e'
- exceptions – 'weird' and 'seize'

LONG AND SHORT VOWEL SOUNDS
- long vowel sounds are 'ay', 'ee', 'eye', 'oh' and 'oo'
- vowels can be made long in various ways: 'e' at the end of a word: e.g 'rat' (*short*), 'rate' (*long*) 'gh' turns 'lit' (*short*) into 'light' (*long*)
- a single consonant mid-word lengthens the vowel before it: spell a person on a bike 'rider', not 'ridder'
- if you video a television programme, you are 'taping' it; if you hear an odd sound, somebody may be 'tapping'
- in these cases, how you say a word is a good guide to spelling

A warning

Spellings of many common words need to be learned individually:

'Though' rhymes with 'go', 'sew', 'snow' and 'beau'. It does not rhyme with 'through' or 'thought' or 'trough', and they do not rhyme with each other.

In this case no rules apply.

38

'-FUL' OR '-FULL'

- descriptive adjectives like 'hopeful', 'cheerful' and 'wonderful' end in a single 'l', although the ending comes from the word 'full'
- when turned into adverbs, the '-ly' ending creates double 'l': 'cheerfully'
- even words like 'cupful' and 'spoonful', which come from 'cup (or spoon) full', have a single 'l'
- note a similar word often misspelt: 'fulfil'

ADDING '-ING'

- you often have to add '-ing' to a verb: 'part' – 'parting', 'shoot' – 'shooting'
- if the verb ends in 'e', remove it: 'taste' – 'tasting', 'time' – 'timing'
- if a short verb ends in a single consonant, it has to be doubled: 'run' – 'running' or 'tap' – 'tapping'
- we spell 'singeing' (*burning*) with an 'e' to avoid confusion with 'singing' (*performing a song*)

SILENT LETTERS

- the most common silent letter is 'k' at the beginning of a word
- be careful with words like 'know', 'knew', 'knot' and 'knight' as the same words exist without 'k' ('now' means 'at this time', 'no' rhymes with 'know')
- sometimes 'g' is treated in the same way as 'k': 'gnat' or 'gnome'
- silent 'p' often comes at the start of much longer words: 'pterodactyl' or 'psychology'
- remember that it is just a silent 'p' at the start of 'psychology' and similar words, not 'ph'
- silent letters in the middle or at the end of words often affect vowel sounds: e.g. 'e' at the end.
- 'gh' is impossible to explain fully: in 'though' it is silent, in 'tough' it makes an 'f' sound

Keep on track

You remember much more of what you read than what you are told. You remember more still if you write it down. During the year keep a spelling list or spelling book of those words you have spelt incorrectly and then have found out (or been told) the correct version. You can use it to check your spelling later and to revise for tests, but simply the act of writing down the words will help.

Be ambitious!

Correct spelling is very important, but nobody expects you to know how to spell every word. Don't be put off using interesting and unusual words because you're not sure about spelling. Spell them sensibly according to the sound, any rules that apply and similar words you know.

Why does this matter?

Accurate spelling is obviously very important. Learning rules helps a great deal (see **Spelling**, pages 38–39), but:

• Frequently the only way to spell a word correctly is to learn it individually.

• These pairs and groups of similar words can be most successfully learned together.

Watch out!

Astonishingly some of these errors have started occurring in newspapers, leaflets, circulars, etc. Join the spelling police: watch out in particular for 'it's'/'its' and 'principle'/'principal'.

✓ In some languages the same letter always produces the same sound. English is not like this, which can often be confusing.

✓ Many words spelt the same sound differently and have different meanings.

✓ Equally, many words share the same pronunciation, but have different spellings.

	Don't confuse		
'The weather will affect (*verb*) my hayfever.'	affect	effect	'the greenhouse effect' (*noun*)
		effect	as a verb, 'effect' has quite a different meaning, 'to make': 'He tried to effect an escape.'
belonging to them short for 'they are'	their they're	there	opposite of 'here'
'I went to London' or 'She's bound to do well in English.'	to	two too	the number 2 in addition: 'He came, too' or more than it should be: 'I'm too lazy.'
'se' is the verb: 'I advise you to practise more.'	advise practise	advice practice	'ce' is the noun: 'My advice is to do more practice.'
a metal: 'lead piping' (*pronounced 'led'*)	lead	led	'The prisoner was led away' – past tense of 'lead' (*pronounced 'leed'*)
past tense of 'pass': 'I passed the test.'	passed	past	time gone by, as 'past tense'
past tense of 'throw'	threw	through	'I walked through the market.'
'Though it looks very similar, it sounds very different!'	though	thorough	careful and diligent: 'a thorough answer'
shortened form of 'it is' or 'it has'	it's	its	belonging to it
shortened form of 'you are'	you're	your	belonging to you

40

	Don't confuse		
'I accept this prize.' 'I expect all to accept their certificates in person, except for those who are ill.'	accept expect	except	'We're all here except William.'
'We don't have access to the staff room.'	access	excess	'excess baggage'
first or chief: 'principal officer' or 'principal' of a college	principal	principle	a rule for living: 'I base my life on Christian principles.'
awake or aware of: 'I became conscious soon after the accident.'	conscious	conscience	feelings of what you ought to do: 'It's on my conscience.'
to make somebody well	heal	heel	parts of the foot (a sole is also a fish!)
to pull something along	tow	toe	
your immortal spirit	soul	sole	

To add to the confusion

There are, of course, words which are spelt and pronounced exactly the same and have totally different meanings (e.g. 'sole'). Think about the different meanings of 'batter', 'kind', 'tender', 'try' and 'felt'.

Keep on track

- There is a temptation to work only on those subjects and parts of the course you find most enjoyable. This is not a good idea.

- However, don't go to the other extreme and ignore those things that you do well. It is important to turn a moderate performance into a good one, but equally so to turn a very good performance into an outstanding one.

To reduce the confusion...

'Batter': beat, or cooking liquid

'Kind': type ('What kind of...?'), or friendly and helpful

'Tender': gentle, or offer ('tender my resignation'), or a small vessel/truck

'Try': attempt, test, or a score at rugby

'Felt': past tense of 'feel', or material

How many similar words can you think of?

Writing

Sentences

Why does this matter?

- Writing a sentence correctly is essential for clear and accurate written English.

- You cannot punctuate correctly if you have difficulty understanding what a sentence is.

- In Speaking and Listening work it is important to use proper sentences in many formal situations (though not in informal talk – see below).

Shortened sentences

'Majorca' is not a sentence, but does it make sense? Yes, in conversation following, 'Where did you go in the summer?', it has become shorthand for 'I went to Majorca in the summer.'

✓ A sentence can be a statement, a question or an exclamation.

✓ The key elements of a sentence are a subject and a verb.

✓ All sentences relate to a particular time: the tense of the verb.

✓ Most sentences contain other elements, but these are the only essentials.

SUBJECT
- a noun or pronoun: 'the book', 'Mr Gryce', 'they'
- the person or thing who is doing or being the verb
- may also contain a word or phrase telling us more about the subject word: 'the <u>thick</u> book' or 'Mr Gryce, <u>with an evil smile</u>'

VERB
- the action of the sentence
- the tense shows the time of the happening: 'He slept' (*past*), 'He sleeps' (*present*), 'He will sleep' (*future*)
- a verb like 'sleep<u>ing</u>' cannot be used as the main verb of a sentence because it does not relate to a particular time: you can say 'He is sleeping' or 'He was sleeping'
- there are also verbs of being that refer to what the subject is, not what it does. The main verb of being is 'to be', but there are others: 'she is worried', but also 'she seems worried' or 'she became worried'

OBJECT
- the person or thing the action is done to, either directly: 'We attacked <u>the enemy</u>', or indirectly: 'She gave <u>the teacher</u> her homework'
- occurs in many sentences, but is not essential like subject or verb
- the last part of a sentence is often not the object
- sentences like 'She ran <u>quickly</u>' and 'He was the <u>last to leave</u>' do not contain objects: nothing is done to anyone or anything

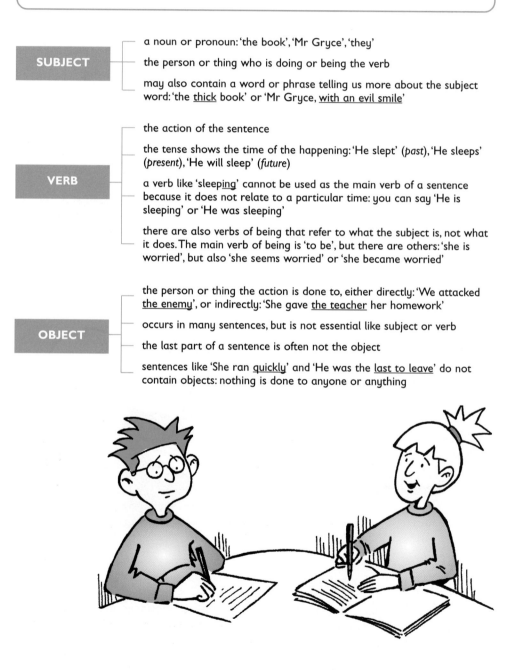

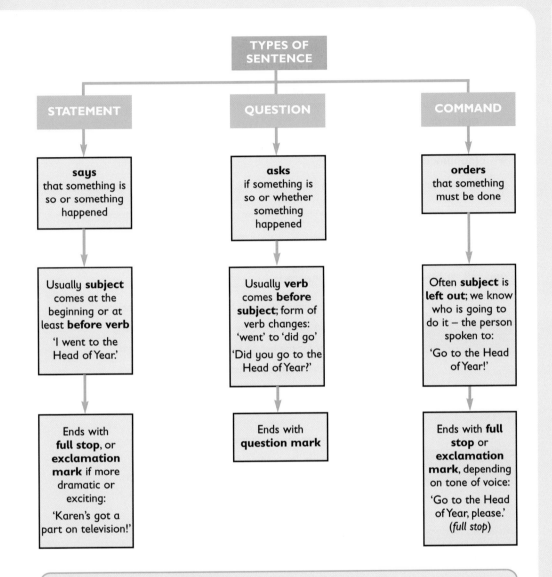

TYPES OF SENTENCE

STATEMENT

says that something is so or something happened

Usually **subject** comes at the beginning or at least **before verb**

'I went to the Head of Year.'

Ends with **full stop**, or **exclamation mark** if more dramatic or exciting:

'Karen's got a part on television!'

QUESTION

asks if something is so or whether something happened

Usually **verb** comes **before subject**; form of verb changes: 'went' to 'did go'

'Did you go to the Head of Year?'

Ends with **question mark**

COMMAND

orders that something must be done

Often **subject** is **left out**; we know who is going to do it – the person spoken to:

'Go to the Head of Year!'

Ends with **full stop** or **exclamation mark**, depending on tone of voice:

'Go to the Head of Year, please.' (*full stop*)

Some notes on word order

- Some (especially old-fashioned) writers place subject after verb for poetic effect. You might read, 'In the morning mist there <u>rose</u> (*verb*) <u>a mighty edifice</u> (*subject*) before our astonished gaze.'

- In English, word order tells us much about meaning. It is dangerous to alter the order of subject and object: 'Dog bites man' and 'Man bites dog' don't mean the same!

- Remember that there can be more parts to a sentence, mostly descriptive words or phrases, so that the subject and verb are surrounded by other words: 'The <u>house stood</u> empty' can become, 'At the end of the street the <u>house</u> with the red front door <u>stood</u> empty for many months.' – 'House' is still the subject; 'stood' is still the verb.

Keep on track

Think of revision as something that happens all the way through the course, not just in the last few weeks (certainly not the last few days or hours!). For instance, 'revision' means 'seeing again' – you cannot do that unless you've seen it clearly the first time.

So every time you miss key work through absence or don't understand the work, make sure that you get hold of it either through notes or asking your teacher.

This is simple!

The sentences on this page are simple sentences. You often read or write longer and more complicated sentences.

Pages 44–45 deal with sentences like this.

Writing

Sentences

Why does this matter?

- Your use of sentences must first of all be correct: this is dealt with on the previous pages.

- Almost as important is that they should be interesting to read. Using simple sentences is fine, but not all the time, so awareness of joining words (conjunctions) matters.

What's in a name?

If you are interested in the correct names:

- sentences with 'and', 'but' and 'so' are compound sentences;

- those with a main statement and less important statements joined by different conjunctions are complex sentences.

Writing

✓ A simple sentence consists of only one statement, question or command.

✓ Joining two or more statements, questions or commands (or a question or command with one or more statements) can be done by various methods.

✓ The simplest is to join together two equal statements by a joining word (conjunction) like 'and'.

✓ More varied sentences can be created by using different conjunctions.

- Conjunctions like 'and', 'but' and 'so' link two equal statements.
- The conjunctions listed below link a less important statement to the main one and tell us how the two are connected.

TIME
- 'When the bus came, I was still on the other side of the road.'
- 'After Sally had eaten lunch, she went over to the library.'
- 'The Head sent for me before I had a chance to explain.'
- 'As the clock chimed, the procession started.'

PLACE
- 'Where the river bends, the boys had set up camp.'

REASON
- 'Kerry was chosen for the team because she was fitter.'
- 'As he was tallest, Jamie lifted down the suitcases.'
- 'Since the other team failed to appear, we went home.'
- Can also use so.

POSSIBILITY
- 'If I pass my exams, I'd like to become a doctor.'
- 'There's no chance of success unless we change our tactics.'

CONTRAST
- 'Though Mark and Paul were friends, they argued all the time.'
- 'Jane said nothing, although she hoped to be chosen for the play.'
- Can also use but.

How does the conjunction change the meaning?

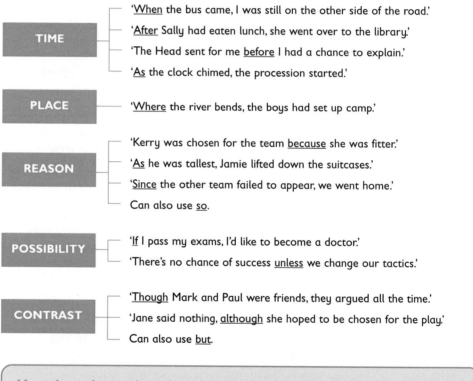

if
unless
I won't go to the club   whenever   Sarah's going to be there.
because
although

Check the different meanings on the opposite page.

Turn two simple sentences into one longer sentence.

'The teacher sat by the window. He watched the pupils outside.'		
Join by 'and', 'but' or 'so' 'The teacher sat by the window **and** watched the pupils outside.'	**Join by another conjunction** '**When** the teacher sat by the window, he watched the pupils outside.'	**Turn one statement into a phrase** '**Sitting by the window**, the teacher watched the pupils outside.'

What is a phrase?

A phrase is any group of words which does not contain a main verb.

'Sitting by the window' is a phrase; so is 'her seat by the window' or even 'by the window.' You can use as many phrases as you like (so long as they make sense and sound good) within a sentence.

'The teacher sat by the window' is a full statement, not a phrase, and needs to be joined to the sentence by a conjunction.

How does the conjunction change the meaning?

if	You're avoiding Sarah and she will be the reason if you don't go.
unless	Sarah is your main reason for going, if you do.
whenever	This is not just one time, you always avoid her.
because	You're avoiding Sarah, and you already know she will be there (and you won't).
although	You'd like to see Sarah, but are not going for some other reason.

Keep on track

Can you learn from essays or stories you have already written during the course?

Sometimes yes, although rereading with no particular aim is a waste of time. Check that you understand why your teacher has made any corrections. Why has he or she inserted punctuation marks or written 'Sentences' in the margin? Then it is worthwhile to write out corrections, making sure that you understand how to avoid the error.

How complex is complex?

Remember that, however good your use of conjunctions, a sentence must not be allowed to get out of control. Extremely long sentences (even correctly put together) can be a problem for the reader.

Writing

Why does this matter?

If you want to write clearly, you must punctuate correctly. Words are not enough; punctuation takes the place of pauses in speech.

'Michael was very excited yesterday afternoon he had seen a fox in the woods.'

What does that mean?

Michael was very excited. Yesterday afternoon he had seen a fox in the woods.

or

Michael was very excited yesterday afternoon. He had seen a fox in the woods.

Don't confuse...

dashes and hyphens.

They look similar, but have different jobs. A hyphen joins together two words to make one: 'lion-hearted', 'white-faced', 'relegation-threatened'. A dash is used to indicate a parenthesis or as an informal way of showing a pause.

✓ There are three punctuation marks that come at the end of a sentence: full stop, exclamation mark and question mark.

✓ There are five punctuation marks that are used within a sentence: colon, semi-colon, dash, brackets and comma.

✓ Speech is shown by the use of ' ' or " ". These marks have a variety of names, all of which are correct: speech marks, quotation marks, inverted commas.

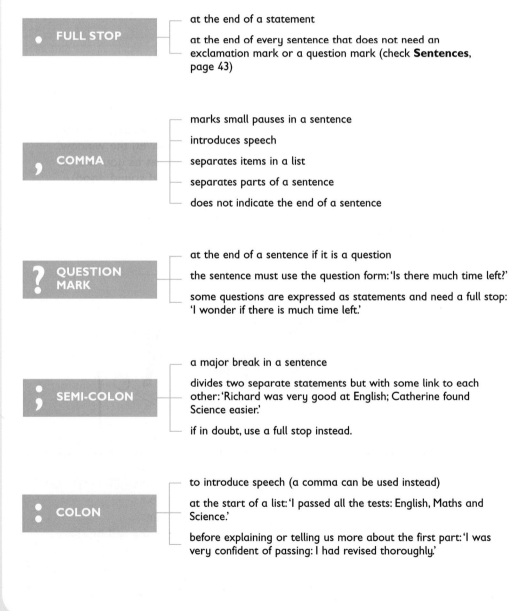

FULL STOP
- at the end of a statement
- at the end of every sentence that does not need an exclamation mark or a question mark (check **Sentences**, page 43)

COMMA
- marks small pauses in a sentence
- introduces speech
- separates items in a list
- separates parts of a sentence
- does not indicate the end of a sentence

QUESTION MARK
- at the end of a sentence if it is a question
- the sentence must use the question form: 'Is there much time left?'
- some questions are expressed as statements and need a full stop: 'I wonder if there is much time left.'

SEMI-COLON
- a major break in a sentence
- divides two separate statements but with some link to each other: 'Richard was very good at English; Catherine found Science easier.'
- if in doubt, use a full stop instead.

COLON
- to introduce speech (a comma can be used instead)
- at the start of a list: 'I passed all the tests: English, Maths and Science.'
- before explaining or telling us more about the first part: 'I was very confident of passing: I had revised thoroughly.'

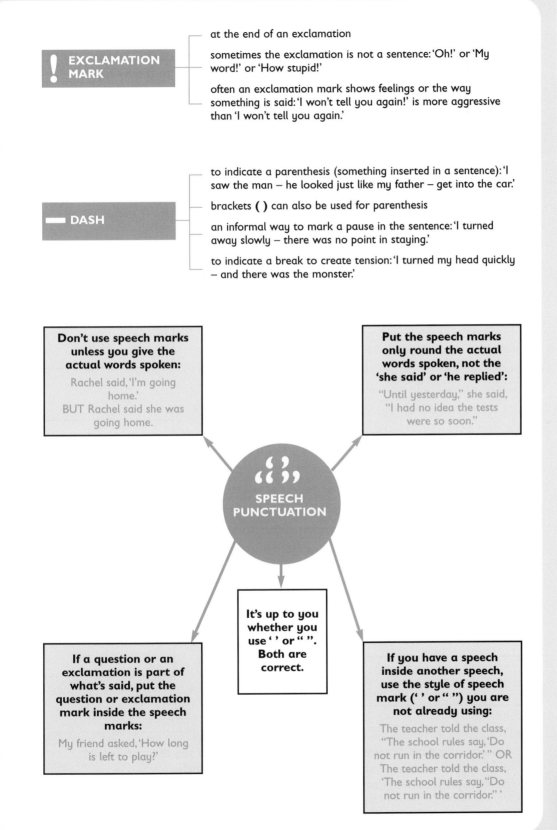

! EXCLAMATION MARK

- at the end of an exclamation
- sometimes the exclamation is not a sentence: 'Oh!' or 'My word!' or 'How stupid!'
- often an exclamation mark shows feelings or the way something is said: 'I won't tell you again!' is more aggressive than 'I won't tell you again.'

▬ DASH

- to indicate a parenthesis (something inserted in a sentence): 'I saw the man – he looked just like my father – get into the car.'
- brackets ( ) can also be used for parenthesis
- an informal way to mark a pause in the sentence: 'I turned away slowly – there was no point in staying.'
- to indicate a break to create tension: 'I turned my head quickly – and there was the monster.'

SPEECH PUNCTUATION

Don't use speech marks unless you give the actual words spoken:

Rachel said, 'I'm going home.'
BUT Rachel said she was going home.

Put the speech marks only round the actual words spoken, not the 'she said' or 'he replied':

"Until yesterday," she said, "I had no idea the tests were so soon."

If a question or an exclamation is part of what's said, put the question or exclamation mark inside the speech marks:

My friend asked, 'How long is left to play?'

It's up to you whether you use ' ' or " ". Both are correct.

If you have a speech inside another speech, use the style of speech mark (' ' or " ") you are not already using:

The teacher told the class, "The school rules say, 'Do not run in the corridor.' " OR
The teacher told the class, 'The school rules say, "Do not run in the corridor." '

Keep on track

You need to work quickly in a test, but not so quickly that the marker is confused by what you write. A sure sign of a rushed essay or story is a lack of full stops and a lack of paragraphs. Don't waste time, but slow down enough to remember to punctuate correctly – especially full stops!

On and on...

If you are writing a very long speech (more than one paragraph), open the speech marks at the start of each paragraph, but do not close them until the very end of the speech.

Why does this matter?

It is important that you use paragraphs to give your writing the shape you want. For example:

- events in the order in which they happened;

- reasons for school uniform followed by those against;

- a story told in flash-back.

Paragraphs for speech

Don't forget that when you are writing conversation, you normally take a new line for a new speaker. This is much clearer for the reader. Sometimes you can manage without putting 'Claire said' or 'James replied' every time.

✓ Paragraphs are essential to divide your writing into clear sections. Start a new paragraph when your writing moves on to a new topic.

✓ Most paragraphs consist of a few sentences on a single topic. However, variety in a paragraph is sometimes helpful.

✓ Indicate a new paragraph by indenting the first line or leaving a gap of a line.

The question that has no answer: 'How long does a paragraph have to be?'

Read the following piece and decide what is gained by the variety in paragraph lengths.

> John felt as if he had been alone in the room for several hours, but in the darkness he had no real idea of the passage of time. If only the guards had not taken his watch! He had explored the room as well as he could: the walls dripping with water, the boarded-up window, the bare wooden bench. He had been left with nothing, no other person to speak to, no means of escape, no way to pass the time before his captors decided what his fate should be. All he could do was rerun the moment when his car was stopped at the check-point and try over and over again to recall some clue to what this was all about and how it might end. All in vain! He started yet again to feel his way round the cell...
>
> Suddenly keys rattled outside and the door swung open.

The first paragraph is far longer than the second paragraph. Why?

In the first paragraph nothing is happening except that John's fear and discomfort are increasing. The writer must not hurry this section.

Suddenly there is action and excitement. The speed is expressed in the short paragraph.

John does not know what the action means: freedom? death? torture? a companion? If the writer resists explaining straightaway, the reader shares John's feelings.

Imagine this as a dramatic scene in a film. Think how the director would pace it and how he or she would use sound. The way the writing is paragraphed conveys something of that effect.

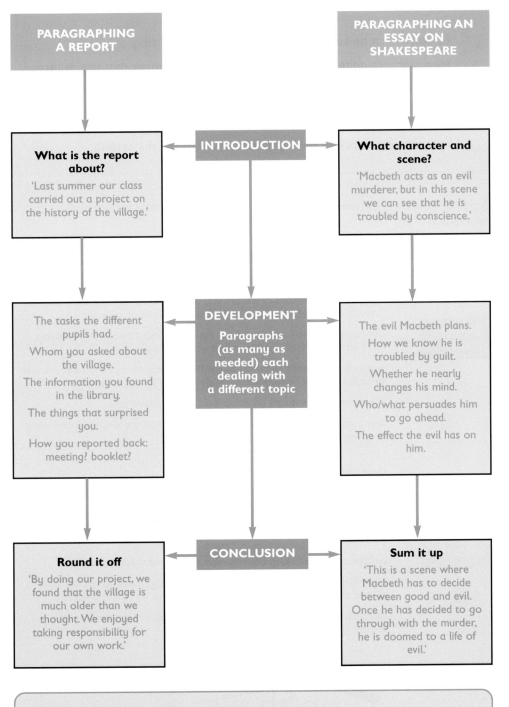

PARAGRAPHING A REPORT

PARAGRAPHING AN ESSAY ON SHAKESPEARE

INTRODUCTION

What is the report about?

'Last summer our class carried out a project on the history of the village.'

What character and scene?

'Macbeth acts as an evil murderer, but in this scene we can see that he is troubled by conscience.'

DEVELOPMENT

Paragraphs (as many as needed) each dealing with a different topic

The tasks the different pupils had.

Whom you asked about the village.

The information you found in the library.

The things that surprised you.

How you reported back: meeting? booklet?

The evil Macbeth plans.

How we know he is troubled by guilt.

Whether he nearly changes his mind.

Who/what persuades him to go ahead.

The effect the evil has on him.

CONCLUSION

Round it off

'By doing our project, we found that the village is much older than we thought. We enjoyed taking responsibility for our own work.'

Sum it up

'This is a scene where Macbeth has to decide between good and evil. Once he has decided to go through with the murder, he is doomed to a life of evil.'

Topic sentences

The first sentence of each paragraph should tell us what the paragraph is about. The plan of the essay becomes clear through these topic sentences.

Keep on track

Remember that what matters most at the end of a revision session is the state of your mind, not how long you've spent or the notes you've made (though these are often helpful). Therefore revising too long without a break can be a waste of time. Concentrate hard; take breaks at preplanned times; set targets of how much you plan to do – and meet those targets.

Ask yourself why

In your reading, try to work out why writers paragraph in the way they do: for instance, in a newspaper article, why does the writer begin with that paragraph? And would a different first paragraph be better?

Mr & Mrs Evans invite you to join them in celebrating their Silver Wedding on March 1st

Writing

Formal and informal language

Why does this matter?

Probably the most common fault in students' writing is to write constantly in the role of a twenty-first century teenager communicating with a friend/parent acquaintance. Don't be pompous in your writing, don't be over-formal, but remember:

- there are many times when formal correctness matters;

- not all the characters in your stories will speak exactly like you.

A manner of speaking

The difference between formal and informal matters in spoken English as well as writing. Don't use the same words and way of phrasing in an informal conversation with friends and a speech to the whole class — and don't speak the same way to your best friend and the headteacher!

Writing

✓ All words can be seen as correct — in the right setting.

✓ Your teachers quite rightly expect you to avoid words that are regarded as offensive.

✓ There is, however, no need to avoid slang — simply avoid using it in the wrong places.

✓ Your task is to choose the right sort of words for the setting.

Types of language (in speech or writing) can be divided into formal and informal.

FORMAL ENGLISH
- polite, correct language
- use the correct form of words: 'I am', not 'I'm'
- if addressing superiors or people you don't know, ask rather than tell: 'I would be grateful if…' and 'please', not 'Send me at once…'
- use correct terms in writing about literature: 'Shakespeare characterises Macbeth as a villain', not 'He makes out that he is evil.'
- sometimes you need technical terms (the correct terms for a certain trade or skill) – 'by-line' (newspapers), 'search engine' (internet) etc.
- take care with sentence construction, tenses, spelling etc.
- avoid colloquialisms (the sort of words you use in conversation) and slang: 'kids' or 'gonna'

INFORMAL ENGLISH
- there are different levels of informality
- the most informal of all is dialogue (conversation) between characters in a story – the speech must reflect the character
- letters to friends or a story told in the first person are also likely to be informal
- colloquialisms and slang are welcome in many of these situations
- there is no excuse for errors of spelling. You may decide to use 'it's' instead of 'it is' and that's fine, but, if you mix up 'its' and 'it's', that's a mistake
- sentence construction still needs to be accurate, unless there's some reason – somebody's speech patterns, perhaps

Where are the misfits?

A formal piece in correct English – is anything too slangy?

Macbeth is plagued by his conscience after he has arranged the murder of Banquo. When Banquo's Ghost appears at the banquet, Macbeth **tells him to shut up and clear off**. None of the lords can see the ghost, so they all assume that Macbeth's **going off his head**.

> How about 'orders him to be silent and leave the hall'?

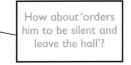

> This one's worse: 'Macbeth is deranged', 'Macbeth is becoming insane', 'Macbeth is losing control of himself' etc.

You are using fairly simple technical language – does anything not fit?

I found the layout of the newspaper very interesting. The bold typeface draws attention to the lead story and they used a lot of **exciting words in big letters at the top**.

> 'Dramatic headlines', or something similar, would be better.

A friendly, informal letter – where are the misfits?

Are you coming over at the weekend? I thought we'd go into town on Saturday morning, then, if you fancy a game of football, there's a field **adjacent to my residence**. Then you could stay for your tea: **I'll request a cooked meal from my parents**.

> How pompous! Try 'by our house'.

> Not quite so pompous, but still formal: 'I'll ask my mum to cook us something.'

Keep on track

In all revision situations the most important consideration is – don't panic!

The way to avoid panic is to prepare.

- Make sure you have everything you need (no books left at school).
- Organise time (no last-minute rush, no clash with the UEFA Cup Final).
- Prepare your work place (if magazines are lying around, you'll start reading them).
- Get yourself ready: an alert mind is the most important part of revision.

To be correct...

The correct term for what this page is about is **register**. You might write in a 'formal register' or 'use the wrong register for the situation'.

Writing

Why does this matter?

'Audience' is all-important in your writing: you must imagine the person(s) sitting there reading your report/story/essay. Is it just meant for your teacher or for someone you know or for the readers of a newspaper?

In the case of a story, think how you can tell it so that the reader:

• is entertained;

• sees things the way you want him or her to: is this character likeable, is this the right way to treat teenagers etc.?

Don't waste space

In most cases, the stories you write are not very long compared to published books. You cannot afford to put in things that don't really matter, so think what you want to achieve and what you need to include to achieve it.

✓ A story should hold the interest of the reader.

✓ This can be done by the narrative method (way of telling a story) you choose.

✓ Characters are as important as events in holding interest.

✓ The order of events is also important: they need not be in the order they occurred.

✓ A story told in the third person (he or she) has a different effect from one in the first person (I).

Here is an idea for a story. What decisions are you going to make to arrange the basic idea into a good story?

Scott is in Year 11 and has problems at school and at home. He is ambitious to do well at school (he wants to be a doctor) and his GCSE examinations are coming up, but he finds it increasingly difficult to get on with one of his Science teachers. This builds up to an incident where he is so rude to his teacher that the Head warns him he might be suspended from school. His parents divorced two years ago and he lives with his mother, who has recently remarried: he doesn't really get on with his stepfather, but there have been no major incidents. Scott is supposed to make sure that his sister, Carly, in Year 8, gets safely on the school bus as they live in a village four miles from the school. But she, too, has been getting on his nerves recently and he pays as little attention to her as possible. Unknown to him, she is finding that life with her stepfather is too much for her and two days before Scott's exams start, she fails to come home from school and disappears. The next day the family decide to call the police...

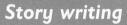

Narrative method

Events in the order in which they happened (chronological order) or flashback, beginning with police bringing news or Carly recovering in hospital.

Two good ideas:

the half-flashback:
begin when they realise she's run away and take the story both forward and back

there are at least two stories here:
Scott and Carly. Why not alternate the two: several paragraphs about what Scott's doing, then a line of asterisks and take up the story of Carly, and so on.

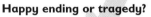

Keep on track

The best (and most enjoyable) way to improve your story writing is to read plenty of well-written, entertaining stories and novels. You don't need to separate learning from pleasure. Enjoy the story, but pay attention to the writer's methods. For example:

* does the flashback method work?

* how well does the narrator's character come across?

* why does he or she change from, say, third person to first person?

Happy ending or tragedy?

Both could work perfectly well, but an ending that is little more than 'They all lived happily ever after' is a bad idea.

If she is found safe, make it clear that Scott, Carly, mother and stepfather all learn something from the events – or fail to.

Are you going to make what happened obvious at first (see **Narrative method**) or use suspense?

Point of focus

You have to decide which character(s) to focus on, but also which events. For instance, are Scott's rows or his exams the main thing, or Carly's home life or what happened when she ran away? All come in the story, but you choose which are most important – and this changes the story.

As it happens

There is nothing wrong with telling your story in chronological order (from the first thing that happened to the last). This is much better than attempting something else and ending up with a confused narrative. But bear in mind that you have the choice – and stop to think and make that choice.

First person narrative?

Unless you choose to tell both stories side by side (and even then you could do it with Scott's and Carly's diaries), a first person narrative is a good idea here because people's feelings are so important ... but who is to tell the story?

Scott's story

What sort of a person is he? This will decide how the story is told. Is he very selfish? He would dwell on the row with the teacher and the nuisance of his sister, with not much about her problems. Maybe, though, he learns how selfish he is and the story is partly about his guilt over Carly.

This links well with flashback: begin with, 'When I saw my sister in the hospital bed, all my so-called problems seemed like nothing.'

Carly's story

This will centre very much on her feelings towards her stepfather. Scott will play quite a small part in the story. In this case we know that she will survive because stories ending 'And then I died' don't work. The ending is not necessarily happy, though: does she look forward to life at home?

Carly's story ties in nicely with the half-flashback: begin, 'It was just after the Easter holidays that I decided I had to run away.'

Mother's story

An interesting challenge: a whole new range of feelings: guilt, self-justification, worry. But she will have a point of view. To Scott and Carly she is not helping them as they think she should, but she has a life (happy?) as well.

Story writing

Why does this matter?

When you write a story, you must interest your reader, but you should also try to control his or her reaction.

• Dialogue adds to interest, but it also tells the reader what to think about the characters.

• The diction you use can tell your reader to laugh/cry/concentrate/become anxious etc.

Try this!

Continue **Story B** until Claire goes to bed. Decide why she goes to bed (sent by father, storms out in fury, just tired) and build your dialogue towards that climax.

> ✓ A story should hold the interest.
>
> ✓ This can be done by your style of writing as well as by your narrative method.
>
> ✓ The use of convincing dialogue (conversation) is important.
>
> ✓ The diction (choice of words) should be suitable for the type of story.

Dialogue: three versions of the same incident

A

Claire knew she was supposed to be home by half past nine, but she missed her bus and found herself with half an hour before the next. So she went back to Alison's house and waited.

Eventually it was well after ten when she arrived home. Her mother and father were waiting in the dining room and she could tell that her father was really angry, though she thought her mother was more upset than annoyed. Her father wanted to know where she had been and seemed to think she had spent the evening with Carl, while her mother worried about the sort of people she might have met at that time of night. After about ten minutes Claire got up and went to bed.

clear   easy to follow   accurately written   boring

B

Claire looked at her watch as she opened the front door – twenty past ten! She decided to put on her most innocent smile and hope for the best.

'Is that you, Claire?' Her mother's voice sounded anxious, but relieved.

'Who else do you think it is? Unless she's brought that Carl back with her!'

Claire opened the dining room door and was halfway through greeting her parents when her father interrupted.

'Do you realise it's nearly half past ten? What sort of state do you think your mother's in? She's been going on for the last half hour about the terrible things that might happen to you.'

'Come on, dad, it's fairly safe at Alison's house.'

'Well, why didn't you phone?' and 'Don't tell me what's safe and what isn't!' shouted her mother and father simultaneously.

clear   characters created   longer than A   much more interesting

Writing

C Claire opened the door timidly and heard her father shouting.

'Where have you been till this time of night?'

'I've only been at Alison's, but I missed the bus.'

'You could have phoned – didn't you have your mobile?'

'Never mind her mobile – don't the Colemans have a phone?'

'Of course they do, but I just forgot. Anyway I didn't think it mattered. After all, it's only just gone ten and Alison's parents never make her come in this early.'

'That's their problem. So long as you're living in this house, you'll stick to our rules.'

'But what if something had happened to you?'

'I'd have used my mobile.'

'That's typical – you never think about using it when your mother's sick with worry.'

lively	*good idea of character*	*longer than A*	*not clear*

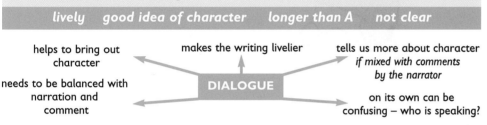

helps to bring out character

makes the writing livelier

tells us more about character *if mixed with comments by the narrator*

DIALOGUE

needs to be balanced with narration and comment

on its own can be confusing – who is speaking?

Diction: two versions of the same event

Suddenly Gregory realised that their right winger had slipped a tackle and had a clear run on goal. He covered as well as he could, <u>desperately aware</u> that, with only minutes left, his team's <u>chances of winning the cup</u> were in <u>danger</u>. He <u>forced</u> himself to <u>concentrate</u>, <u>stood firm</u> against the attacker, then dived to his right as the shot came in. <u>Too late</u>: the ball was in the net and <u>the school's hopes</u> were over for another year.

Suddenly Gregory <u>came out of his dream</u> of saving a penalty at Wembley to hear the <u>crowd (three Year 7s)</u> shouting at him. He saw the winger charging towards goal and tried to narrow the angle – <u>unfortunately geometry was never his best subject</u>! The winger <u>scuffed</u> his shot, Gregory <u>dived dramatically</u> in the <u>wrong direction</u> and the ball <u>trickled slowly</u> over the line.

The diction tells the reader:

take this seriously	*treat this as a comic event*

Keep on track

You have probably read or heard far too much about exam stress. This not only makes you miserable, it's actually unhelpful in your work, so get rid of it if at all possible.

Revise hard, but, if you are behind in your revision, just think:

- if you spend your time worrying about what you have to do, you do nothing;

- if you realise you won't complete your revision, get down to work and only do 75 per cent of it: this is better than trying to rush through it all.

Make it clear!

The more dialogue you use, the more important it is to punctuate speech correctly. There is a section on speech punctuation in **Punctuation** (page 47).

Writing

Why does this matter?

- Even with e-mails, faxes and telephone, much of our business is conducted by letter.

- In a large crowded office, mail is less likely to go astray if you follow the rules about using names, addresses, dates etc.

- A clear, firm, polite letter is always more likely to get the response you want.

Suit yourself!

You will see many letters where the exact placing of addresses, dates etc. is different from this model. It doesn't matter whether your address is lined up to the left or right, or where exactly you place the date or the name and address you are writing to, but the same details should be there.

✓ There are two sorts of letter: formal and informal.

✓ An informal letter is one that you would write to a friend (or penfriend) or a relation.

✓ For an informal letter you can largely make your own rules, though address, date and 'Dear…' are usual. The important thing is to be interesting.

✓ A formal letter needs to be written according to the rules: writing to a local business, applying for tickets, booking a holiday, asking for information from your MP etc.

Remember:

- Be clear.
- Be firm.
- Be polite.
- Be well organised.
- Use paragraphs sensibly.
- Bear in mind that this letter will be read and filed in an office, probably without its envelope. That is why the rules of layout (dates, names, addresses) are so important.

A formal letter

This layout can change in detail, but should include the same information.

Don't include your name.

Not really necessary with post codes, but many like to include it.

Using the name is a good idea; if not, try to address your letter to the job (The Site Manager, The Booking Office, Customer Relations etc.), not just the firm.

15, Greenhill Avenue,
Bradford,
West Yorkshire
BD3 1QV

14th June 2000

Mr B Sanderson,
Holidaze Mobile Homes,
Sandcliff Road,
Brighton
BN9 7WW

(or 'Dear Sir' or 'Dear Madam', if you don't know the name)

Dear Mr Sanderson,

I am interested in booking a mobile home for four people on your site from July 27th to August 4th this year.

Make clear at the beginning what your business is.

Second paragraph: *your* requirements

I would like to know what facilities there are, both in the caravans themselves and on site: in particular, whether there are any bar and restaurant facilities. Also, although I have seen a brochure for 1999, **I would be grateful if you could send me** an up-to-date list of charges.

Be polite, though firm!

Third paragraph: what are *the reader's* requirements?

If required, I would be happy to send a deposit in advance if we decide to go ahead with the booking. I should also mention that we are likely to arrive very late on the evening of July 27th and that we will be bringing a dog – a small well-behaved Yorkshire terrier. **If either of these is likely to cause a problem, please let me know**.

Polite again!

I look forward to hearing from you and receiving your scale of charges and I hope that you will be able to confirm availability for those dates.

Round it off, remind the reader of what you want, and keep up the politeness.

Yours sincerely,

G. Benson

G. Benson

('Yours faithfully', if you've used 'Sir' or 'Madam')

Some people think it's smart to have an illegible signature: it isn't! Printing your name below is a good idea, though.

Keep on track

Be comfortable with your revision. Choose a place and times where you can relax and concentrate, but do not take relaxation too far. It is helpful to settle into a comfortable chair in good light with all your books and notes to hand. It is helpful to take short breaks. It is not helpful to keep half an eye on the television while pretending it helps your concentration.

Dear Sir...?

What do you use if you don't know whether the person you are writing to is male or female? The old rule was to write 'Dear Sir'. These days 'Dear Sir or Madam' is more likely to be used.

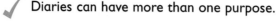

Why does this matter?

- You need to be able to write in as many forms as possible: first and third person narratives, factual reports, etc. The diary form is useful for both factual (holidays, work experience etc.) and fictional (suspense stories, diaries of prisoners etc.) writing.

- There are many books in diary form that you might either study or read for pleasure, e.g. the diaries of Anne Frank (fact) or Adrian Mole (fiction).

What style?

Is there a special style of writing for a diary?

Not as such, but you may wish to leave out small words like 'I' and 'the' in a personal diary – do not overdo it, though!

✓ Diaries can have more than one purpose.

✓ Using diaries to note appointments or as a check on your actions is useful, but not part of your English studies.

✓ Diaries can record both your activities and your feelings.

✓ The key point about a diary is that it records events and emotions day by day, not at the end of the story.

WHO IS THE DIARY WRITTEN FOR?

the writer?	the public?	the family?	posterity?

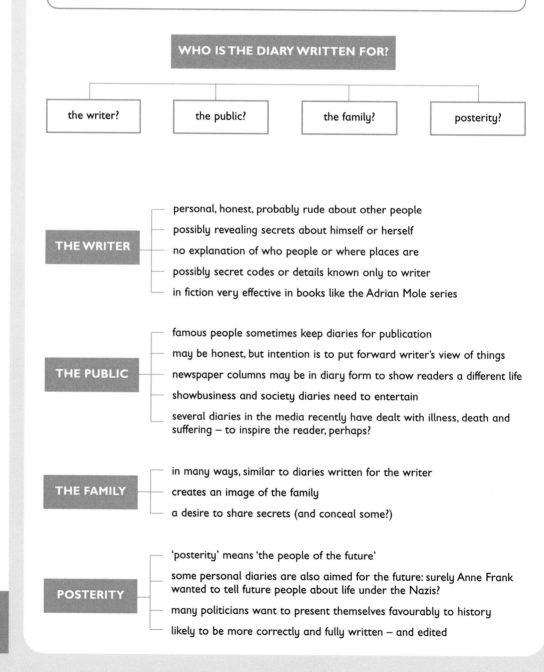

THE WRITER
- personal, honest, probably rude about other people
- possibly revealing secrets about himself or herself
- no explanation of who people or where places are
- possibly secret codes or details known only to writer
- in fiction very effective in books like the Adrian Mole series

THE PUBLIC
- famous people sometimes keep diaries for publication
- may be honest, but intention is to put forward writer's view of things
- newspaper columns may be in diary form to show readers a different life
- showbusiness and society diaries need to entertain
- several diaries in the media recently have dealt with illness, death and suffering – to inspire the reader, perhaps?

THE FAMILY
- in many ways, similar to diaries written for the writer
- creates an image of the family
- a desire to share secrets (and conceal some?)

POSTERITY
- 'posterity' means 'the people of the future'
- some personal diaries are also aimed for the future: surely Anne Frank wanted to tell future people about life under the Nazis?
- many politicians want to present themselves favourably to history
- likely to be more correctly and fully written – and edited

Writing

Your own stories: when is diary form suitable?

In a diary there is a daily cut-off. If you have been worried by possible intruders and terrified by strange noises, you cut off the story when you go to bed or phone the police or sit down with a shotgun and a cup of coffee to wait. Then you begin again:

> Today confirmed my worst fears. I got up early after a sleepless night and was shocked to discover...

or

> This morning dawned bright and fresh and I found it hard to imagine my fears of last night...

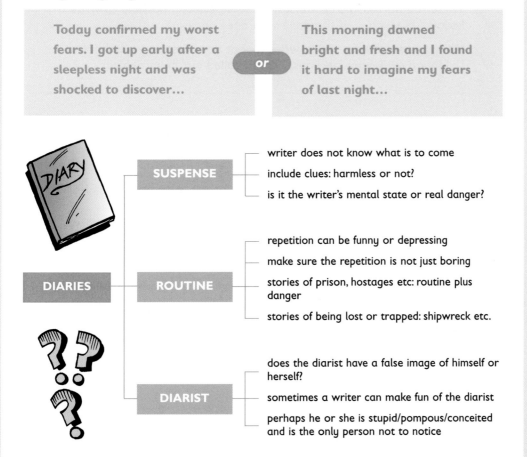

DIARIES

SUSPENSE
- writer does not know what is to come
- include clues: harmless or not?
- is it the writer's mental state or real danger?

ROUTINE
- repetition can be funny or depressing
- make sure the repetition is not just boring
- stories of prison, hostages etc: routine plus danger
- stories of being lost or trapped: shipwreck etc.

DIARIST
- does the diarist have a false image of himself or herself?
- sometimes a writer can make fun of the diarist
- perhaps he or she is stupid/pompous/conceited and is the only person not to notice

Keep on track

Be prepared for whatever your tests may ask of you. You will probably not be asked to write a diary extract in the SATs, but make sure that you know the form required of every sort of writing: diary, report, letter, newspaper article etc. Don't plunge into a piece of writing without thinking about what form is needed.

Try this!

It may be that you keep a diary yourself. In that case, the reader it is aimed at is you and you will decide how it is written. But why not see how interestingly you can express yourself? Make it an entertaining read for yourself!

A classic fictional diary

G. and W. Grossmith wrote *The Diary of a Nobody* over a hundred years ago. The 'nobody' was Mr Pooter, who, sadly, thought he was 'somebody'. Read this example of his 'sense of humour' and see how the Grossmiths mock their character.

> **May 26. Left the shirts to be repaired at Trillip's. I said to him: 'I'm 'fraid they are frayed.' He said, without a smile: 'They're bound to do that, sir.' Some people seem to be quite destitute of* a sense of humour.**
>
> * lacking

Why does this matter?

A large amount of your writing consists of stories about yourself. They need to be well planned and interesting.

- Decide what sort of person you are (or were when the events took place).

- Share your emotions (excitement/fear/ amusement/ happiness) with the reader.

- Decide on the way you want to present events to hold the reader's interest.

See yourself...

Honesty about yourself is a virtue in such writing. See things from your own point of view, but recognise that you are selfish/ vague/irritable/ demanding. This is easier to do when looking back at the 'you' of five or ten years ago.

✓ A book telling the story of someone's life is called a biography.

✓ If it is written by the person who is the subject of it, it is called an autobiography.

✓ These are normally true stories, but it is perfectly possible to write a fictional biography of someone who does not exist.

✓ Many pieces you are set to write (about your first day at school or childhood memories, perhaps) can be called autobiographical.

Autobiographical writing is about two things: the events and yourself.

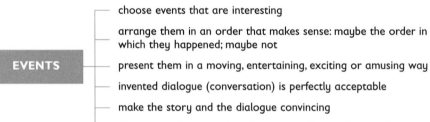

EVENTS
- choose events that are interesting
- arrange them in an order that makes sense: maybe the order in which they happened; maybe not
- present them in a moving, entertaining, exciting or amusing way
- invented dialogue (conversation) is perfectly acceptable
- make the story and the dialogue convincing
- if you are asked to write a longer autobiography, use chapters or separate sections on specific topics

YOURSELF
- you are not just writing about events; you are creating a picture of yourself: think about the sort of person you are/were
- start by suggesting how the story is typical/unusual and relates to your character
- remember it is your story: if events are seen only from your point of view, that is fine
- you do not have to understand other people's actions, but it is interesting to comment later on what you have found out
- other characters should be made as interesting and 'alive' as possible, but can reflect the way you saw them as a child; e.g. First Day at School – make the teacher as terrifying as you wish, but you might write, 'Later I found Mrs Saunders was…'

How to start a piece of autobiographical writing:

MY FIRST HOLIDAY ABROAD

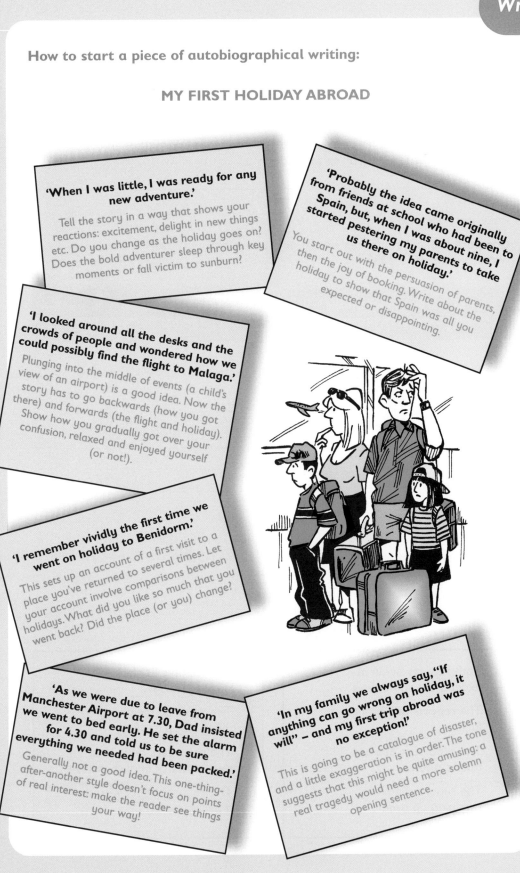

'When I was little, I was ready for any new adventure.'

Tell the story in a way that shows your reactions: excitement, delight in new things etc. Do you change as the holiday goes on? Does the bold adventurer sleep through key moments or fall victim to sunburn?

'Probably the idea came originally from friends at school who had been to Spain, but, when I was about nine, I started pestering my parents to take us there on holiday.'

You start out with the persuasion of parents, then the joy of booking. Write about the holiday to show that Spain was all you expected or disappointing.

'I looked around all the desks and the crowds of people and wondered how we could possibly find the flight to Malaga.'

Plunging into the middle of events (a child's view of an airport) is a good idea. Now the story has to go backwards (how you got there) and forwards (the flight and holiday). Show how you gradually got over your confusion, relaxed and enjoyed yourself (or not!).

'I remember vividly the first time we went on holiday to Benidorm.'

This sets up an account of a first visit to a place you've returned to several times. Let your account involve comparisons between holidays. What did you like so much that you went back? Did the place (or you) change?

'As we were due to leave from Manchester Airport at 7.30, Dad insisted we went to bed early. He set the alarm for 4.30 and told us to be sure everything we needed had been packed.'

Generally not a good idea. This one-thing-after-another style doesn't focus on points of real interest: make the reader see things your way!

'In my family we always say, "If anything can go wrong on holiday, it will" – and my first trip abroad was no exception!'

This is going to be a catalogue of disaster, and a little exaggeration is in order. The tone suggests that this might be quite amusing: a real tragedy would need a more solemn opening sentence.

Keep on track

Revision is not just a matter of how long you spend on a task. If you leave it till late, you might be too tired. If you divide your attention between revision and television, TV will get more than 50 per cent.

What matters is how much you remember, so, at the end of a revision session, give yourself a quick test.

Other people

Have you read any autobiographies? Roald Dahl's is very entertaining and shows how you can exaggerate without losing the basic truth of events.

Writing

Why does this matter?

You need to be able to write in many different styles, including factual accounts. See how newspapers write their reports in a way that makes it easy for readers to pick up the main points and try to do the same when you are asked to present a report on something.

Reading papers

Three questions to ask yourself about a newspaper (local or national):

Does it

- report clearly and well?
- hold the reader's interest?
- make its views obvious?

If it does all three, it's a good model for you.

✓ For any report, organisation is crucial.

✓ It is important to let the reader know at the beginning what the report is about.

✓ Then a reporter must select and use his or her information in a way that makes the story clear to the reader.

Fact and opinion

Compare the first sentences of two newspaper reports covering the same two stories in June 2000.

A Eurostar train derailed – all passengers escape...	Reporters look forward to the Test series against the West Indies...
Hundreds of terrified British passengers had an astonishing escape last night when their Eurostar train derailed at almost 200 mph. (*Mail*)	Nasser Hussain conceded yesterday that England are now underdogs for the coming series against the West Indies. (*Mail*)
A Eurostar train came off the tracks at 200 mph yesterday, but miraculously none of the 500 passengers was badly hurt. (*Mirror*)	Pour a stiff drink, draw the curtains, have a good scream. England are still favourites to beat the West Indies. (*Mirror*)

Both reports begin in exactly the same way.

The reports are giving facts.

The reporters are not taking sides.

The reports begin by summing up events.

The reports begin in opposite ways.

The reports are giving different opinions.

The reporters have their own views of English cricket.

The reports begin with the main opinion.

You may be asked to write a newspaper-style report, either just giving facts or expressing an opinion based on facts.

STATE THE MAIN POINT CLEARLY AT THE BEGINNING

- say what the subject of the story is (as in the Eurostar accounts)
- **or**
- express your opinion (as in the cricket stories)

- do not start listing events with no explanation: 'The Eurostar train left Paris at 5.30' is not the way to start

MAKE SURE YOU USE FACTUAL DETAIL IN THE STORY

- give details of the people: names, ages, occupations etc.

- use quotations from people involved, eye-witnesses, relatives etc.

- avoid phrases like 'a man who saw what happened'

- if necessary, use words like 'eye-witness', 'spokesperson' or 'representative'. The *Mail* has a quotation from 'a spokesman for France's SNCF railways'

KEEP YOUR STORY CLEAR – AVOID CONFUSION

- paragraphs should be fairly short – in newspapers they are often one sentence, but you can make them a bit longer

- sentences should be about one thing only

- group facts on the same subject together: e.g. keep separate the details of how the crash happened, quotations from relatives, information on reopening the line and interviews with rail chiefs

> **Remember**
>
> **Your report on the school football team should begin:**
>
> Hillcrest School came back from 3-0 down at half time to force a dramatic draw against Downwood High.
>
> **not**
>
> Hillcrest School kicked off and the first attack ended when the Downwood goalkeeper saved a good shot from Alan Powell.

Keep on track

You can help your memory by using mnemonics. These are sayings or rhymes that help to fix things in your memory. 'I before **e** except after **c** when the sound is **ee**' is one. So is the sentence '**R**ichard **O**f **Y**ork **G**ave **B**attle **I**n **V**ain' to remind you of the colours of the spectrum. But you can make up your own – no matter how silly.

Try this!

Do you have a school magazine or a class newspaper? If not, perhaps you could start one. Then you could write reports on sports fixtures, plays, new teachers, field trips etc.

Making notes

Why does this matter?

- Taking notes is an essential skill, one that you already need and that you will need even more for GCSE.

- To do it successfully, you must always remind yourself that notes are in every way an abbreviated (shortened) form.

Just for you!

Notes are just for you, so any abbreviations, symbols and squiggles are all right so long as you understand them. Keep them as short as possible, but make sure you can read them!

✓ Notes are brief versions of the original.

✓ There is no need to write sentences in full.

✓ Work out what is essential or at least important.

✓ Use abbreviations: 'wk' for 'week', 'subj' for 'subject', 'diffic' for 'difficult' etc.

Making notes for a piece of continuous writing

What do you think is the importance of sport in education? Do you think there should be more or less sport in schools?

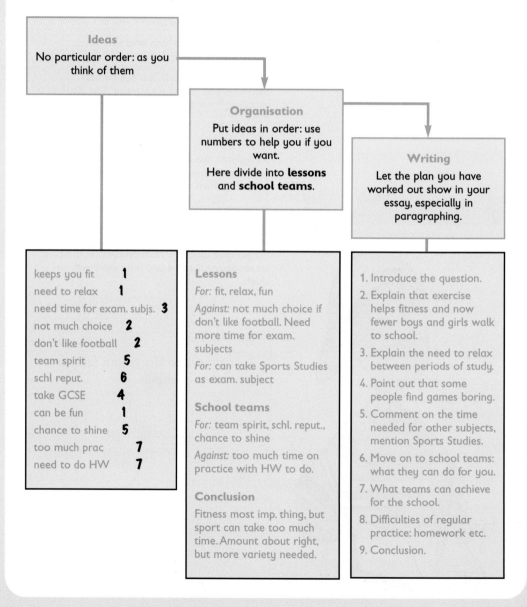

Ideas
No particular order: as you think of them

Organisation
Put ideas in order: use numbers to help you if you want.
Here divide into **lessons** and **school teams**.

Writing
Let the plan you have worked out show in your essay, especially in paragraphing.

keeps you fit	1
need to relax	1
need time for exam. subjs.	3
not much choice	2
don't like football	2
team spirit	5
schl reput.	6
take GCSE	4
can be fun	1
chance to shine	5
too much prac	7
need to do HW	7

Lessons

For: fit, relax, fun

Against: not much choice if don't like football. Need more time for exam. subjects

For: can take Sports Studies as exam. subject

School teams

For: team spirit, schl. reput., chance to shine

Against: too much time on practice with HW to do.

Conclusion

Fitness most imp. thing, but sport can take too much time. Amount about right, but more variety needed.

1. Introduce the question.

2. Explain that exercise helps fitness and now fewer boys and girls walk to school.

3. Explain the need to relax between periods of study.

4. Point out that some people find games boring.

5. Comment on the time needed for other subjects, mention Sports Studies.

6. Move on to school teams: what they can do for you.

7. What teams can achieve for the school.

8. Difficulties of regular practice: homework etc.

9. Conclusion.